HMH Florida Science

FLORIDA STATEWIDE SCIENCE ASSESSMENT (FSSA) REVIEW AND PRACTICE

GRADE 7 STUDENT BOOKLET

Houghton Mifflin Harcourt

Introduction

To the Student

This booklet is designed to help you prepare to take the Florida Statewide Science Assessment (FSSA). The table of contents at the beginning of this book shows how the book is organized. The first section of the book contains review material and practice questions that are grouped by topic. Following the review material and practice questions is a practice test. The practice test is followed by an answer sheet for recording your answers for the test.

When you take the FSSA, you will be tested on the designated Science Benchmarks. Each of the Benchmarks that you may be tested on is included in the review and practice section. Reading the short review of each concept, and then answering the practice questions that follow, will be a good way to check your understanding of the material.

Taking the practice test will also help you prepare for the FSSA. The practice test should be similar to the FSSA test that you will take. After taking the practice test, you may find that there are concepts you need to review further.

Test Taking Tips

General Tips

- Read the directions carefully before you begin.

- Budget your time based on the number and type of questions. Set aside time to recheck your answers after you're done.

- When using a separate answer sheet, use a ruler or blank sheet of paper as a guide to avoid marking answers on the wrong line.

- If there is no penalty for guessing, it's better to guess than to leave an answer blank.

- Guess well, not wildly. Try to eliminate one or two answer choices first.

- Read the question fully and carefully. Many students miss the correct answer because they read only part of the question, and choose an answer based on what they think the question is asking.

- In the question stem, note key terms that tell you what to look for in the answer choices: What? When? Where? What NOT? What kind? How many?

If you encounter a question about a key term or vocabulary term that is unfamiliar to you, try to break the word up into word parts. If you know what part of the word means, you may be able to eliminate some answer choices.

Using Images

Tables and Graphs
- Read the title.

- Note the units of measure.

- For tables, read row and column headings.

- For graphs, note the data points.

- For graphs, read the axes labels.

- Look for trends and patterns.

Diagrams
- Read the title and all labels.

- Do not rely on relative sizes of items to compare size. Look for a scale.

- BEFORE you look at the diagram, read the question all the way through. Look for hints in the question that will tell you what to look at in the diagram.

- AFTER reading the question, read and look through the whole diagram to understand what it illustrates, and what processes or parts are involved.

- Follow numbered steps in order or trace arrows to understand a process.

- Look at the diagram's parts and then see how they work together.

Maps
- Read the title, key, place names, and names of other map features.

- Note the scale, compass direction, and location of important features with respect to one another.

Using Reference Sheets
- Before beginning the test, look at the reference sheets to see what is included.

- During the test, when a question addresses a topic included on the reference sheet, look at the reference sheet after you read the question.

Question Types

Multiple Choice Questions

- Read the whole question and answer it on your own before you read the answer choices.

- Read all the answer choices before you choose one.

- Read each answer choice along with the question.

- Eliminate any obviously wrong choices.

- Look for words that limit your choices, such as "most" or "best" which may indicate that there are probably several correct answers, but you should look for the one that is the most important, or had the most effect.

- If two responses are opposites, one of them is likely correct.

- Answers that include words such as **sometimes** or **often** are more likely to be correct.

Multi-Step Multiple Choice Questions

- It may not immediately be clear that a question is a multi-step problem. Read through the whole question and think about what you would need to do in order to answer the question.

- Break down the problem into the steps you would need to take in order to find the answer based on the information given in the question.

- What is the relationship between the information given and the question you are asked to answer?

- What is the useful information in the question that you will need? How many steps are necessary to get from the information to the answer?

- Outline the steps on scratch paper. Then work through each step as needed on the scratch paper. Find your answer before going back to the answer choices with the problem.

- What is the main topic of the problem? Have you answered problems on that topic before? If so, what strategies worked for you before?

Formulas

$$\text{Density} = \frac{\text{mass}}{\text{volume}} \qquad\qquad D = \frac{m}{V}$$

$$\text{Average speed} = \frac{\text{total distance}}{\text{total time}} \qquad\qquad s = \frac{d}{t}$$

$$\text{Net force} = (\text{mass})(\text{acceleration}) \qquad\qquad F = ma$$

$$\text{Work} = (\text{force})(\text{distance}) \qquad\qquad W = Fd$$

Periodic Table

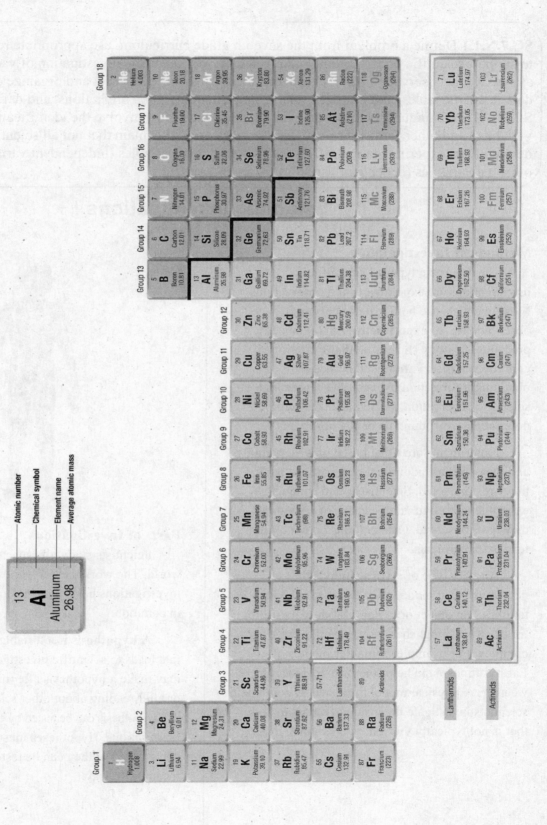

SC.7.N.1.1 Define a problem from the seventh grade curriculum, use appropriate reference materials to support scientific understanding, plan and carry out scientific investigation of various types, such as systematic observations or experiments, identify variables, collect and organize data, interpret data in charts, tables, and graphics, analyze information, make predictions, and defend conclusions. **SC.7.N.1.3** Distinguish between an experiment (which must involve the identification and control of variables) and other forms of scientific investigation, and explain that not all scientific knowledge is derived from experimentation. **SC.7.N.1.4** Identify test variables (independent variables) and outcome variables (dependent variables) in an experiment.

Scientific Investigations

Methods of Investigation

The two basic types of scientific investigations are experiments and observations. Most scientists use both experiments and observations. An **experiment** is an organized procedure to study something under controlled conditions. **Observation** is the process of obtaining information by using the senses. In a scientific observation, a scientist takes careful notes about everything he or she observes.

Experiments are often based on observations, and they produce additional observations while they are conducted. Scientists often conduct experiments to find out the cause of something they have observed. Observations do not always lead to experiments.

Another type of investigation is the development of models. Models are representations of an object or system. Models are useful for studying things that are very small, large, or complex. For example, computer models of Earth's atmosphere help scientists forecast the weather. A physical model for instance, could help scientists investigate the inside of a human body that is not typically viewed by the human eye.

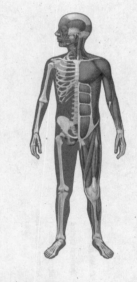

Parts of Investigations

Scientists study all aspects of the natural world. The work they do varies, but their investigations have some basic elements in common.

A **hypothesis** is a testable idea or explanation that leads to scientific investigation. A scientist may make a hypothesis after making observations or after reading about other scientists' investigations. The hypothesis can be tested by experiments or observations. Hypotheses must be carefully constructed so they can be tested in a practical and meaningful way.

Variables are factors that can change in a scientific investigation. An **independent variable**, or test variable, is the factor that is deliberately manipulated in an investigation. The hypothesis determines what the independent variable will be. An experiment should have exactly one independent variable. Scientists try to keep all other variables in an experiment constant, or unchanged, so they do not affect the results. A **dependent variable**, or outcome variable, is the factor that changes as a result of manipulation of one or more independent variables.

Data are pieces of information gathered by observation or experimentation. Data can be used in calculating or reasoning. Scientists analyze data to determine the relationship between the independent and dependent variables in an investigation. Then they draw conclusions about whether the data supports the investigation's hypothesis.

Scientific Methods

Conducting experiments and other scientific investigations is not like following a cookbook recipe. Scientists do not always use the same steps in every investigation or use steps in the same order. They may even repeat some of the steps. Even though the methods used in different investigations may vary, all scientists use some common methods. These may include:

- Defining a problem: A scientific problem is a specific question that a scientist wants to answer. The problem must be well-defined, or precisely stated, so that it can be investigated.

- Forming a hypothesis and making predictions: When scientists form a hypothesis, they are making an educated guess about a problem. Before testing a hypothesis, scientists usually make predictions about what will happen in an investigation.

- Planning an investigation: Scientists need to decide how to conduct an investigation, what equipment and technology are required, and how materials for the investigation will be obtained.

- Identifying variables: The independent variable of an experiment is identified in the hypothesis. Scientists must also identify other variables that will be controlled.

- Collecting and organizing data: The data collected in an investigation must be recorded and properly organized so that they can be analyzed. Data such as measurements and numbers are often organized into tables, spreadsheets, or graphs.

- Analyzing and interpreting data: After they finish collecting data, scientists must analyze this information. Their analysis will help them draw conclusions about the results.

- Drawing and defending conclusions: Scientists conclude whether the results of their investigation support the hypothesis. When they publish the results of their investigation, scientists must be prepared to defend their conclusions if they are challenged by other scientists.

Evaluating Scientific Information

The standards for scientific investigations are rigorous. Experiments should be verified through repetition and replication. Before a report on an investigation is published in a scientific journal, it should undergo a peer review by scientists not involved in the investigation. These checks help ensure that good scientific practices are followed.

Student-Response Activity

1 A scientist is interested in studying how tomatoes grow. What is a testable hypothesis that the scientist could investigate?

_____

_____

2 How are observations and experiments similar and different? Complete the Venn diagram to answer.

Experiment

Both

Observation

3 What is the difference between the independent variable and the dependent variable in an experiment?

_____

_____

_____

4 Why might a scientist conduct an experiment in the lab, and then repeat the experiment in the field?

_____

_____

_____

5 What are at least five different methods scientists might use in an investigation?

_____

_____

_____

Benchmark Assessment SC.7.N.1.1, SC.7.N.1.3, SC.7.N.1.4

Fill in the letter of the best choice.

1 Steps in a scientific investigation vary, but must follow a logical sequence. Which list shows the **best** sequence for steps in a scientific investigation?

(A) analyze data, defend conclusions, define a problem, form a hypothesis

(B) analyze data, form a hypothesis, define a problem, defend conclusions

(C) define a problem, form a hypothesis, analyze data, defend conclusions

(D) form a hypothesis, define a problem, defend conclusions, analyze data

2 Experiments have both test variables (independent variables) and outcome variables (dependent variables). Which describes a test variable (independent variable)?

(F) A scientist carefully notes all of the conditions in the environment while observing bald eagles.

(G) A scientist investigating frog behavior alters the temperature in a frog's environment.

(H) A scientist observes that plants that receive red and blue light grow faster than those that receive yellow light.

(I) A scientist performing an experiment on plant growth makes sure that temperature and soil conditions are the same for all plants.

3 Which choice **best** describes a testable hypothesis?

(A) Carrots look better when given more water.

(B) Lilacs are better smelling than roses.

(C) Mountain lions travel over 100 km per day.

(D) The bacterium *E. coli* is worse than the bacterium *S. aureus*.

4 A scientist raises the temperature of a sample of water to find out if the amount of salt that can be mixed into the water changes. Which is the outcome variable (dependent variable)?

(F) the temperature of the water

(G) the amount of water in the sample

(H) the type of salt mixed into the water

(I) the amount of salt that mixes in the water

5 Scientists investigate questions in different ways. Which **best** describes an experiment?

(A) A biologist watches a single herd of elephants over several months.

(B) A climate scientist put data into computer programs to make predictions.

(C) An astronomer uses specialized tools to gather data about distant galaxies.

(D) A physicist puts an object into a vacuum chamber and measures how fast it falls.

SC.7.N.1.2 Differentiate replication (by others) from repetition (multiple trials).

Replication and Repetition

How Science Is Validated

A scientist performs an investigation and draws a conclusion about whether or not the results support a hypothesis. If the hypothesis is supported, what should the scientist do next? The temptation may be to announce the results to the scientific community, but it would be much too soon. The results of a single investigation do not supply enough evidence to validate the hypothesis. A hypothesis can be better validated by being retested.

There are two ways that scientific investigations can be retested. First, the scientist who conducted the original investigation can repeat the study. This is called **repetition**. Multiple repetitions of an investigation with similar results provide support for the findings. Second, other scientists can **replicate** the investigation, or perform the exact same experiment as the first scientist. Reproduction of the findings by different scientists in different locations also provides support.

Repetition

The first step to confirm the results of an investigation is to repeat the study. Multiple repetitions of an investigation that produce similar results can provide support for the findings. For example, suppose you follow a recipe to bake a cake. The first cake is delicious so you decide to bake another one. Unfortunately, the next cake does not taste the same. You were not able to repeat the results from the first cake. It might be that you did not follow the recipe as you had the first time, or maybe the temperature of your oven was not the same as it was the first time. You cannot confirm that the cake recipe is a good one until it can be used to produce the same delicious cake at least three times.

A similar process occurs in science. Suppose a scientist wants to track the growth rate of the bacterium *E. coli* at different temperatures. The scientist may put samples of the bacteria onto petri dishes and observe their growth rates under different conditions.

Growth rate of *E. coli*

Temperature (°C)	Time to double size of bacteria colony (minutes)
10	220
15	110
20	45
25	30
30	22

The scientist analyzes the results and draws a conclusion that it takes less time to double the bacteria colony as the temperature increases. Before the scientist should consider the conclusion valid, he or she must conduct the same experiment several more times. If multiple experiments produce similar results, the scientist can consider the results to be reliable.

Replication

Replication is another way to confirm the results of an investigation. Before results can be considered valid, many different scientists must be able to replicate the investigation and obtain similar results. Scientists must carefully describe the procedure so that anyone can follow it. As long as they have a procedure, other scientists should be able to repeat the investigation. Reproduction of the findings by different scientists in different locations will show that the experiment was valid.

Think again about the cake example. Suppose you made the recipe three times and the results were the same each time. You give the cake recipe to a friend. Unfortunately, your friend's cake does not taste as good as yours. Your friend was not able to replicate your results. It might be that your friend did not follow the recipe exactly as you had, or maybe your friend's oven was slightly hotter than yours. Whatever the reason, you cannot confirm that the recipe is a good one until someone else uses it to produce the same delicious cake.

Think again about the *E. coli* investigation described earlier. If another scientist tries to replicate the investigation, he or she needs to repeat the procedure in the same exact way as in the original experiment. The scientist will need to use the same size and type of petri dish, the same amount of nutrients, and the same variety of *E. coli*. If the scientist does everything in the same way and gets the same results, it can help validate the results.

If the second scientist replicates the *E. coli* investigation, but gets different results, he or she will need to find out why. It could be because the first scientist made an error. It could also be that the second scientist changed some aspect of the investigation. Or it could be that some other factor neither scientist had considered affected the experiment. The process of doing science requires that every possibility be considered. That is why it is important for scientists to repeat and replicate investigations.

Student-Response Activity

Read about the botanist's experiment, and then answer Questions 1–2.
A botanist sets up an experiment by putting two identical plants in identical pots. She then puts the pots in a special case together so that all environmental conditions are the same for each plant. The botanist gives one plant only water. She gives the other water plus nutrients. The botanist gives each plant the same amount of water each day for thirty days and measures the growth of the plants. She finds that the plant that received water plus nutrients grew twice as fast as the plant that received only water. The botanist concludes that the nutrients help the plant grow faster.

❶ How could repetition be used to validate the botanist's results?

_____

_____

_____

❷ How could replication be used to validate the botanist's results?

_____

_____

_____

3 How are repetition and replication similar to and different from each other? Complete the Venn diagram to show your answer.

Repetition

Both

Replication

4 A scientist gets a surprising result from an experiment. Another scientist fails to get the same result after multiple attempts. What should the scientists conclude?

_____
_____
_____
_____
_____

Benchmark Assessment SC.7.N.1.2

Fill in the letter of the best choice.

1 Which choice does **not** describe replication?

(A) Two astronomers observe an eclipse from different observatories.

(B) Two scientists both perform experiments on the same species of plant.

(C) A scientist reads a journal article, and then does the experiment it described.

(D) A scientist shares a procedure with another scientist who then does the experiment.

2 A scientist describes an experiment as follows:

Two identical plants were grown in identical conditions, except one received fertilizer and water while the other received only water. The plant that received fertilizer grew faster.

Which **best** describes why the experiment either can or cannot be replicated?

(F) The experiment can be replicated because the results were indicated.

(G) The experiment can be replicated because both plants had identical conditions.

(H) The experiment cannot be replicated because no two plants are exactly the same.

(I) The experiment cannot be replicated because the methods are not fully explained.

3 Repetition and replication are important methods for validating scientific results. Which **best** describes why?

(A) Repeating and replicating investigations can show if scientists make errors.

(B) Repeating and replicating investigations gives more scientists a chance to work.

(C) Repeating and replicating investigations takes time and effort, but are necessary.

(D) Repeating and replicating investigations allows the public to decide if the results are valid.

4 Which describes repetition?

(F) A chemist measures the timing of a chemical reaction several times.

(G) A large-scale experiment is conducted by a team of several scientists.

(H) One scientist tells another scientist about the results of an experiment.

(I) A scientist looks at data from an experiment and interprets it in a new way.

5 Which is **not** an example of repetition?

(A) Susan makes a baked pasta recipe for the second time.

(B) Frank conducts an experiment already done by Rico on soil bacteria.

(C) Casey tests her slug experiment for a third time.

(D) Bryan tests his physics experiment again in the same day.

SC.7.N.1.5 Describe the methods used in the pursuit of a scientific explanation as seen in different fields of science such as biology, geology, and physics. **SC.7.N.3.2** Identify the benefits and limitations of the use of scientific models.

Representing Data

Methods in Different Scientific Fields

When investigating a scientific question, it is important to use appropriate methods and tools. The method you use to gather scientific information can also vary across different fields of science. Methods of gathering evidence can be done in the field or in the laboratory. Fieldwork gives scientists the opportunity to collect data in an original setting. Biologists and geologists do fieldwork. Conditions cannot be controlled in the field. A biologist might observe how animals behave in their natural environment. They may look at how the animals gather food or interact with other animals.

In the laboratory, scientists can collect data in a method that is controlled. A chemist for instance might be trying to see how two substances react with each other. A physicist might study the energy of a new laser.

Earth Science Methods

Scientific methods allow Earth scientists to learn about species that died out millions of years ago. One team of scientists found dinosaur fossils in the Sahara Desert. They found a set of jaws 1.8 meters (6 feet) long. They could tell from the shape of the jaws and teeth that it was not from a dinosaur. They also knew that rivers once flowed through this now extremely dry region. The team hypothesized that the jaws belonged to a giant crocodile that lived in rivers. To support their hypothesis, the scientists needed more data. They later found skulls, vertebrae, and limb bones. They assembled about half of a crocodile skeleton and compared the bones to modern crocodiles. The scientists concluded that the fossils supported their original hypothesis.

Scientific Models

Scientists use information they have gathered to make models. A scientific **model** is a visual or mathematical representation of an object or a system. Models are useful for showing things that are too small, too large, or too complex to see easily. Models are used in science to help explain how something works or to describe how something is structured. Models can also be used to make predictions or explain observations. Some examples of scientific models include physical models, mathematical models, and conceptual models.

To be truly useful, a model must be in proportion with the object it represents. So, a model must have a scale that relates to the object, much like a map has a scale that relates to actual distances. A model must also be accurate. Otherwise, it will be misleading. Even when models are accurate, they have limitations because it is never exactly like the real thing it represents. For example, a model of a cat may show the parts of the body, but does not act like an actual body of a cat would. Even so, the model is useful for understanding how the parts of a body are related.

Physical Models A physical model is one that you can touch and see. A toy rocket, a dollhouse, and a plastic skeleton are examples of physical models. Drawings and diagrams are also physical models. Many physical models look like the thing they represent, but may not represent every aspect of it.

a weather forecast model can show areas of temperatures and winds at various distances on a map. By relating mathematical calculations on weather data, scientists can predict what areas will experience certain weather and when.

Conceptual Models A conceptual model is a description of an idea. For example, the idea that life originated from chemicals is a conceptual model. This type of model develops an idea based on reasoning and evidence and may include other types of models to express information.

Mathematical Models A mathematical model may be made up of numbers, equations, and other data. Some of these models are fairly simple and can be used easily. Other mathematical models are more complex, and require computers to make and manipulate them. For example,

Student-Response Activity

1 Why would a scientist's method of data collection change based on where they conduct their experiment?

_____

_____

_____

_____

2 Robbie uses a foam ball the size of a basketball and paint to make a model of Earth's layers. List two limitations of the model.

_____

_____

_____

_____

_____

Name ______________________ Date ____________

Benchmark Review
SC.7.N.1.5, SC.7.N.3.2

3. How might methods and models used in physics differ from those used in geology?

____

____

____

____

____

____

4. Why are models used in science?

____

____

____

____

____

____

Benchmark Assessment SC.7.N.1.5, SC.7.N.3.2

Fill in the letter of the best choice.

1 Which is a benefit of a scientific model?

(A) It provides a complete image of the concept it is modeling.

(B) It provides an accurate scale of the concept it is modeling.

(C) It provides an accurate visual representation of the texture and coloring of the concept it is modeling.

(D) It provides a useful understanding of the concept it is modeling.

2 A Punnett square is a type of model.

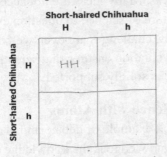

Short-haired Chihuahua

Short-haired Chihuahua

H   h

H   HH

h

Which type of model does this Punnett square represent?

(F) conceptual

(G) functional

(H) mathematical

(I) physical

3 Which is an advantage of conducting an experiment in a laboratory?

(A) All experiments can be successfully conducted in a laboratory.

(B) Conditions are not controlled which allow useful variability.

(C) It is a controlled method of data collection.

(D) The results are better than in a field experiment.

4 Which subject of a science experiment would **not** be useful to have a physical model included?

(F) a human heart

(G) an animal cell

(H) an equation on forces

(I) the solar system

5 What makes a model **not** useful?

(A) if it is in proportion with the object it represents

(B) if it is made of a different material than the object it represents

(C) if it is not the same mass of the object it represents

(D) if it is out of proportion with the object it represents

SC.7.N.1.6 Explain that empirical evidence is the cumulative body of observations of a natural phenomenon on which scientific explanations are based. **SC.7.N.1.7** Explain that scientific knowledge is the result of a great deal of debate and confirmation within the science community. **SC.7.N.2.1** Identify an instance from the history of science in which scientific knowledge has changed when new evidence or new interpretations are encountered.

Basing Scientific Explanations on Evidence

Empirical Evidence

Scientists are curious. They look at everything going on around them and ask questions. They collect any information that might help them answer these questions. Scientific knowledge is based on **empirical evidence**. It is all the measurements and data scientists gather in support of a scientific explanation. Scientists get empirical evidence in many different places. Generally, scientific work is categorized as field or laboratory work.

Reliability of Scientific Knowledge

Scientific knowledge gives us the most reliable methods of understanding nature. Scientific knowledge and discoveries are long-lasting and reliable due to the ways in which they are developed. It takes time for new ideas to develop into scientific theories or to become accepted as scientific laws. In this way, scientific knowledge that scientists question today has formed over hundreds, or even thousands, of years.

An idea is only considered a scientific one if it can be tested and supported by evidence. The process of building scientific knowledge never ends as it can change over time as discoveries and new data continue to raise questions. As a result, scientists explore these questions. If their answers do not support the original idea, then the idea must change. Scientists should always use scientific methods to test new ideas.

Scientific Debate

Most scientists do not work in isolation. They collaborate and share ideas. In a way, all scientists are trying to solve a puzzle. Often, many brains are better than one when solving a puzzle. Scientists regularly gather at meetings to discuss and debate ideas. This helps them to come to an agreement on their ideas. Many ideas are not accepted at first. It is the nature of science to question every idea. Many times, challenges are even welcomed. This rigorous evaluation ensures that scientific knowledge is solidly supported.

New Evidence with Atoms

A good example of debate and change in scientific knowledge is the knowledge of atoms. By the mid-1800s, most scientists agreed matter was made of atoms. However, they were not sure what atoms looked like. At first, they thought atoms probably looked like tiny, solid marbles. They assumed atoms of different substances probably differed by their masses. Later empirical evidence suggested that atoms most likely contained even smaller parts. Scientists observed that these smaller parts carried electric charges and that most of an atom's mass was concentrated at its center. Scientists still saw atoms as extremely small and still often treated them like they were tiny marbles. They came to realize, however, that to explain how atoms interact in the best way, they needed a more complex picture of them.

Today, scientists are still trying to refine the picture of the atom. Much of what they do involves literally smashing atoms into one another.

They examine the patterns made by the crashes. As this new scientific knowledge arises, it allows scientists to change their preexisting knowledge of atoms.

Atoms being Smashed Together

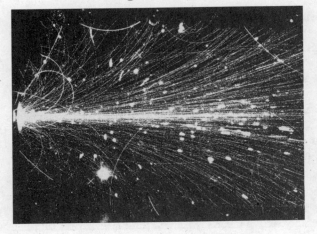

New Evidence in Astronomy

The study of astronomy also illustrates how scientific knowledge can change over time. Almost everything the earliest astronomers knew about the universe came from what they could discover with their eyes and minds. The Greek philosopher, Ptolemy, thought that Earth was at the center of the universe and that the other planets and the sun revolved around it. Then, in 1543, Copernicus published a theory that the sun is at the center of the universe and all planets—including Earth—orbit it. His theory was based on observations he made of the movement of the planets.

In 1609, Johannes Kepler proposed that all planets revolve around the sun in elliptical orbits, and that the sun is not in the exact center of the orbits. He used data he had collected about the positions of the planets at different times as evidence to support his argument. In 1687, Isaac Newton stated that all objects in the universe attract each other through gravitational force and explained why all the planets orbit the most massive object in the solar system—the sun. Based on the work of Kepler and others, Newton developed a very accurate model of the solar system.

Evidence Shapes Scientific Knowledge

Newton's ideas were tested over and over again. All the observations scientists made and data they gathered from experiments were empirical evidence. Because all the evidence supported Newton's ideas, they were unchanged for hundreds of years. Newton's law of gravity remained unchanged until the twentieth century. In 1915, Albert Einstein published his theory of general relativity. Einstein showed that gravitation depended not only on mass and distance, but on time as well. Einstein also realized that gravity is caused by the distortion of space and time. While Newton's ideas about gravitation are still used today to perform basic calculations, Einstein's ideas have allowed scientists to make much more precise and accurate calculations when studying extremely massive objects.

Student-Response Activity

1 Why is scientific debate of knowledge beneficial?

_____

_____

_____

_____

_____

2 A geologist has dug up remains of a prehistoric type of saber-toothed cat and is working out in the field to excavate more remains. What evidence might the scientists be trying to gather?

_____

_____

_____

_____

3 What might a biologist look for to collect evidence about the life of a squirrel in its natural habit?

_____

_____

_____

_____

4 Why does scientific knowledge change throughout time? Provide an example to support your claim.

_____

_____

_____

_____

Benchmark Assessment SC.7.N.1.6, SC.7.N.1.7, SC.7.N.2.1

Fill in the letter of the best choice.

1 Which **best** describes empirical evidence?

Ⓐ It is based on scientific knowledge.

Ⓑ It is the mathematical portion of data scientists gather in support of a scientific explanation.

Ⓒ Scientific knowledge is based on empirical evidence.

Ⓓ You cannot get it in many places.

2 Which describes how scientists gain scientific knowledge?

Ⓕ Most scientific knowledge is accepted right away by scientists.

Ⓖ Most scientists work in isolation.

Ⓗ They rarely use scientific methods to test new ideas.

Ⓘ They work in collaboration and share ideas.

3 What would happen if scientific knowledge was not debated and confirmed by scientists?

Ⓐ More ideas would become theories.

Ⓑ Scientific knowledge would not be supported.

Ⓒ Scientific knowledge would be more accurate.

Ⓓ Scientific knowledge would be easier to understand by nonscientists.

4 Which **best** describes scientific knowledge?

Ⓕ It stays the same over time.

Ⓖ It is not always a reliable method of understanding nature.

Ⓗ It can change over time and builds off of new evidence and data.

Ⓘ It takes a short amount of time for scientific knowledge to develop into theories and laws.

5 Which example is **most likely** to cause scientific knowledge to change?

Ⓐ A scientist tested a plant experiment and did not get the exact same results as the current scientific knowledge suggests.

Ⓑ One scientist decides that current knowledge on a species is incorrect.

Ⓒ New evidence and machines allow scientists to get a more in-depth look at cancer.

Ⓓ Scientists out west have experienced a shorter fall season this year and thus conclude that scientific knowledge on seasons needs to change.

SC.6.N.2.2 Explain that scientific knowledge is durable because it is open to change as new evidence or interpretations are encountered.

Scientific Knowledge

Scientific Knowledge

Scientific knowledge gives us the most reliable methods of understanding nature. Scientific knowledge and discoveries have lasting effects on humanity and the world. Science is reliable and long lasting because of the ways in which it is developed. Being reliable and long lasting, however, does not mean that scientific knowledge does not change. In fact, part of what makes knowledge scientific is its ability to change in light of new information. An idea is only considered a scientific one if it can be tested and supported by evidence. Scientists' ideas are often called into question by new discoveries and data. Scientists then explore the questions the new discoveries raise. If the answers to the new questions do not support the idea, then the idea has to change.

History shows that new scientific ideas take time to develop into theories or to become accepted as facts or laws. Scientists should be open to new ideas, but they should always test those ideas with scientific methods. If new evidence contradicts an accepted idea, scientists must be willing to re-examine the evidence and re-evaluate their reasoning. The process of building scientific knowledge never ends. In this way, the scientific ideas that people investigate today are extensions of ideas that people have been investigating for hundreds, or even thousands, of years.

Changes in Theories

Good scientific knowledge does not always last forever. Theories and models often change with new evidence. Thus, the best scientific theories and models are those that are able to adapt to explain new observations. The theory of light is an interesting example of how scientific knowledge can adapt and change. Scientists debated the theory of light for some time. At one time, scientists saw light as particles, and later they saw it as waves. The wave theory, however, seemed to explain more about light. For a long time, scientists accepted it.

Today, however, scientists view light as having both a particle nature and a wave nature. In a sense, the particle theory of light did not die. It was good scientific knowledge. It was just incomplete. Most scientists today would probably agree that all scientific knowledge is incomplete. Even the best theories do not explain everything. Indeed, this is the reason science continues. The goal of science is best described as the attempt to explain as much as possible and to be open to change as new evidence arises. As you study science, perhaps the best advice to remember is that everything we know about the world is simply the best guess we have made. The best scientists are those who are open to change.

Refraction in the particle theory of light

Reflection in the wave theory of light

Interpretations Change Thought

Scientific knowledge about astronomy is another good example of how scientific thought changes over time. Almost everything that the earliest astronomers knew about the universe came from what they could discover with their eyes and minds. The Greek philosopher Ptolemy thought that Earth was at the center of the universe and that the other planets and the sun revolved around Earth. Then, in 1543, Copernicus published a theory that the sun was at the center of the universe and that all of the planets—including Earth—orbit the sun. He based his theory on observations he made of the movement of the planets. In 1609, an astronomer named Johannes Kepler proposed that all of the planets revolve around the sun in elliptical orbits and that the sun is not in the exact center of the orbits. Data he collected about the positions of the planets at different times supported his argument. In 1687, Isaac Newton showed that all objects in the universe attract each other through gravitational force and explained why all of the planets orbit the most massive object in the solar system—the sun. By using the work of Kepler and others, Newton was able to develop a very accurate model of the solar system.

Combined Evidence Helps Form Ideas

Isaac Newton made many contributions to multiple fields of mathematics and science. His ideas about gravity, for example, helped to shape scientific thought for hundreds of years. Newton's law of gravitation states that all matter in the universe exerts an attractive force on all the other matter in the universe. It also states that the strength of that force depends on the masses of the objects, which are attracting each other, and on the distance between them. In 1798, more than one hundred years after Newton first described the law of gravitation,

a scientist named Henry Cavendish accurately measured the gravitational constant. Newton's ideas and the evidence gathered by Cavendish enabled people to accurately predict the motion of objects in our solar system.

Newton's law of gravitation stood exactly as he first described it in 1687 until the twentieth century. Then, in 1915, Albert Einstein published his theory of general relativity. Einstein showed that gravitation depended not only on mass and distance, but on time as well. Einstein also realized that gravity is caused by the distortion of space and time. Newton had been thinking in three dimensions; Einstein introduced the fourth. By examining all of the evidence, reasoning logically, being open to change, and using creativity, Einstein was able to come up with a new and improved explanation of how the universe works. Einstein's ideas have allowed scientists to make much more precise and accurate calculations when studying extremely massive objects.

Student-Response Activity

1 What are two scientific ideas that have changed throughout time? Explain why the ideas changed.

_____

_____

_____

_____

_____

_____

❷ Long ago, people thought that lightning never struck the same place twice. Over time, our understanding of weather events has changed a lot. Give at least two reasons why our understanding of lightning might have changed so much.

_____

_____

_____

_____

_____

❸ Maria thinks that scientific knowledge never changes. Explain why Maria is incorrect and why it would be negative if scientific knowledge never changed.

_____

_____

_____

_____

_____

❹ Why does good scientific knowledge not last forever?

_____

_____

_____

Benchmark Assessment SC.6.N.2.2

Fill in the letter of the best choice.

1 Which **most likely** allowed Einstein's theory of general relativity to be an accepted piece of scientific knowledge?

Ⓐ He had a greater level of education than Newton.

Ⓑ He had an ability to examine evidence and be open to change.

Ⓒ He was not open to change or new interpretations.

Ⓓ His idea was more complex than previous ideas.

2 Which is **true** about scientific knowledge?

Ⓕ It can never be disproven.

Ⓖ It is often complete.

Ⓗ It is often incomplete.

Ⓘ It is never debated.

3 Which is the **least important** factor in deciding whether an idea is a valid scientific idea?

Ⓐ data from observations or experiments

Ⓑ if it can be repeated

Ⓒ if it is able to be replicated

Ⓓ the length of time that an idea has been around

4 In the 1800s, some scientists believed in the "rainfall follows the plow" idea, which was that breaking prairie sod would allow rainfall to be absorbed into the soil and this moisture would evaporate, causing an increase in rainfall. Which would **most likely** lead to this scientific idea being disproven and revised?

Ⓕ a few people not believing in the idea any longer

Ⓖ documentation of heavy rainfall in the 1800s in prairies

Ⓗ severe droughts and improved climate data in the 1800s

Ⓘ taller crops being grown in the 1800s than in the 1700s

5 What is the **longest** amount of time scientists might investigate a scientific idea?

Ⓐ a couple of years

Ⓑ a few days

Ⓒ fourteen hours

Ⓓ hundreds or thousands of years

SC.7.N.3.1 Recognize and explain the difference between theories and laws and give several examples of scientific theories and the evidence that supports them.

Theories versus Laws

Nature of Scientific Knowledge

You may think that what you find out in science is accepted by everyone and unchanging. That is not always true. The "facts" of science are simply the most widely accepted explanations. Scientific knowledge is and probably always will be changing. To understand the nature of scientific knowledge, you must understand how scientists use certain words. *Law* and *theory* are two familiar words that have very specific scientific meanings.

Defining Laws

A scientific **law** is a description of a specific relationship under given conditions in the natural world. Scientific laws describe the way the world works. They are scientific principles that work without exception to predict or explain nature under specific conditions.

Laws are typically statements, which can be written as mathematical equations. The law of conservation of energy states that energy in a system can neither be created nor destroyed. This is fairly easy to understand conceptually. Another example of a law is Boyle's law, which states that the pressure and volume of a gas are inversely proportional. Boyle's law can be written mathematically as $pV = C$, meaning that the pressure of a gas multiplied by its volume will always give the same value (the constant C).

Even though *law* may sound better established or more concrete than *theory*, laws are still subject to change. Newton's law of gravitation, for example, was considered to be complete until Einstein introduced his theory of relativity.

Defining Theories

While laws describe what happens, scientific theories attempt to explain how things happen. A scientific **theory** is an explanation supported by a large body of evidence. Theories can be used to help us understand the laws we observe. Most scientists agree theories are the best explanations based on what we know now.

Theories are based on lots of evidence and are widely accepted. A theory, though, is subject to change and improvement. Theories are continuously investigated with new questions and subjected to testing against new evidence. Scientists recognize that theories are incomplete. Still, theoretical knowledge is complete enough to allow human beings to understand, predict, and manipulate the natural world.

The kinetic theory of gases for example, can explain Boyle's law. The kinetic theory describes a gas as being composed of quickly moving particles. The particles of gas constantly bounce off of the walls of the container they occupy. The pressure of the gas increases the more frequently the particles bounce off the sides of the container.

Darwin's Theory of Evolution

The scientific theory of evolution is another example of a theory. Evolution is the process in which inherited characteristics within a population change over generations, sometimes giving rise to new species. When Charles Darwin first wrote about evolution by natural selection, he did not know about the laws of inheritance or the molecular basis of traits.

As scientists have learned more about these two fields of study, they have improved upon Darwin's explanation for how species change over time.

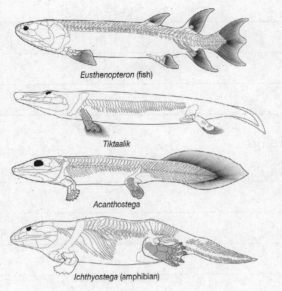

Eusthenopteron (fish)

Tiktaalik

Acanthostega

Ichthyostega (amphibian)

Much of the evidence supporting the scientific theory of evolution comes from the fossil record. As paleontologists have uncovered more fossils, a more complete set of data has become available, allowing scientists to revise the theory of evolution. For example, fossil evidence of an aquatic organism named *Tiktaalik,* supported that it had both fish and amphibian characteristics and evolved from fish ancestors. Today, scientists understand that there are many intricacies in how species evolve, and not all scientists agree on exactly how evolution occurs. Nearly all scientists agree, though, that the theory of evolution accurately explains how new species have appeared on Earth over time.

Student-Response Activity

 What is one example of a theory or law and how did scientists gain evidence to support it?

_____

_____

_____

_____

_____

❷ Why is it important to understand how scientists use the words **law** and **theory**?

_____

_____

_____

_____

_____

Name _____ Date _____

3 Diego states that he has a scientific theory on why people yawn. How is he using the word **theory** incorrectly in a scientific context?

_____
_____
_____
_____
_____

4 How is a scientific law different from a scientific theory?

_____
_____
_____
_____
_____
_____
_____

Benchmark Assessment SC.7.N.3.1

Fill in the letter of the best choice.

1 Which is an example of a scientific theory?

(A) A scientist explains that the area of a rectangle is proportional to the width times the length, or A = wl.

(B) A scientist explains that the force acting on an object is equal to the mass times the acceleration, or F = ma.

(C) A scientist thinks a purple moth and butterfly are the same species because they look alike.

(D) Scientists agree that Earth's axis is tilted. This explains why there are seasons.

2 Which is an example of a scientific law?

(F) Leo sees a group of individuals get sick after drinking water near his town, and he concludes that all the water in the area is contaminated.

(G) Scientists agree it requires energy to break down food. This explains why your body temperature changes when you are digesting food.

(H) Scientists agree that in asexual reproduction, 100% of the DNA from the parent is transferred to the offspring.

(I) Scientists agree that polar bears would not do well in a desert environment because their bodies are designed to keep heat in.

3 How do theories and laws relate?

(A) Laws and theories are the same concept.

(B) Laws are used to help us understand the theories we observe.

(C) Theories and laws are used to contradict each other.

(D) Theories can be used to help us understand the laws we observe.

4 Which is a drawback of theories?

(F) Few scientists take theories seriously.

(G) They are never tested.

(H) They are subject to change and are still incomplete.

(I) They have little support backing them.

5 An architect needs to know how much mass a material can withstand before it cracks, to use it as the base of a five-story building she is designing. She uses a proven formula to calculate the amount of material needed and mass it can withstand. Which **best** describes how the architect can know the right amount of mass?

(A) She uses a law, because it is a proven formula.

(B) She uses a law, because the calculations are based on evidence.

(C) She uses a theory and law, because it is a real world problem.

(D) She uses a theory, because she can explain the effects of force and mass on materials.

SC.7.E.6.1 Describe the layers of the solid Earth, including the lithosphere, the hot convecting mantle, and the dense metallic liquid and solid cores. **SC.7.E.6.5** Explore the scientific theory of plate tectonics by describing how the movement of Earth's crustal plates causes both slow and rapid changes in Earth's surface, including volcanic eruptions, earthquakes, and mountain building. **SC.7.E.6.7** Recognize that heat flow and movement of material within Earth causes earthquakes and creates mountains and ocean basins.

Earth's Layers

Inside the Earth

If you were able to cut Earth in half, you would notice that Earth is made up of several layers. Each layer of Earth has its own properties and composition. When studying the chemical composition of Earth's layers, scientists have identified three main layers—the crust, mantle, and core. The crust is the outer layer of Earth and the layer where living things live and grow. There are two types of crust: continental and oceanic. Continental crust makes up the continents, while oceanic crust makes up the oceans.

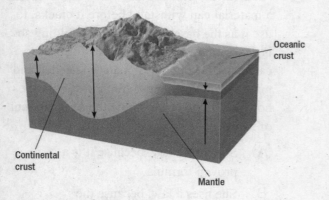

Earth's Layers

The mantle is located between the crust and core. It is made of hot, slow-moving, solid rock. Convection causes cooler, denser rock to sink and warmer, less dense rock to rise. When warmer rock rises and is closer to Earth's crust, scientists are able to study the rock and learn more about Earth's mantle.

The core is located beneath the mantle and the center of Earth, and is likely made of the metals iron and nickel. The core is very hot and very dense. It makes up about one-third of Earth's mass.

The Earth has five main layers. They are the lithosphere, asthenosphere, mesosphere, outer core, and inner core. The outer layer of Earth is called the **lithosphere**. It is made up of the crust and the rigid, upper part of the mantle. This layer is divided into moving tectonic plates. The **asthenosphere** is a layer that contains softer parts of the mantle and is made up of rock that moves slowly. The **mesosphere** is the lower part of the mantle. Like in the asthenosphere, rock in this layer flows slowly. The rock in the mesosphere flows even more slowly than the rock in the asthenosphere. The outer core is a liquid layer located beneath the mantle. This layer surrounds the inner core, which is the solid center of Earth.

Plate Tectonics and Earth's Layers

The theory of plate tectonics describes large-scale movements of Earth's lithosphere. Plate tectonics explains how and why features in Earth's crust form and continents move. The lithosphere, or the solid outer layer of Earth, is divided into tectonic plates that move in different directions and different speeds. Each plate fits together with the plates surrounding it. The plates all vary in size, shape, and thickness. The Andes Mountains, for instance, formed where the South American plate and Nazca plate meet.

Plate Boundaries

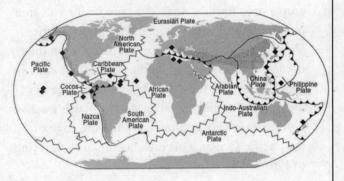

Plate Boundaries

A **plate boundary** is where two tectonic plates meet. The most dramatic changes in Earth's crust occur along plate boundaries. Plate boundaries may be on the ocean floor, around the edges of continents, or even within continents. There are three types of plate boundaries: divergent boundaries, convergent boundaries, and transform boundaries. Each type of plate boundary is associated with characteristic landforms.

Convergent boundaries form where two plates collide. Three types of collisions can happen at convergent boundaries. When two tectonic plates of continental lithosphere collide, they buckle and thicken, which pushes some of the continental crust upward. When a plate of oceanic lithosphere collides with a plate of continental lithosphere, the denser oceanic lithosphere sinks into the asthenosphere. Boundaries where one plate sinks beneath another plate are called subduction zones. When two tectonic plates of oceanic lithosphere collide, one of the plates subducts, or sinks, under the other plate.

At a **divergent boundary**, two plates move away from each other. This separation allows the asthenosphere to rise toward the surface and partially melt. This melting creates magma, which erupts as lava. The lava cools and hardens to form new rock on the ocean floor.

A boundary at which two plates move past each other horizontally is called a **transform boundary**. However, the plate edges do not slide along smoothly. Instead, they scrape against each other in a series of sudden slippages of crustal rock that are felt as earthquakes. Unlike other types of boundaries, transform boundaries generally do not produce magma. The San Andreas Fault in California is a major transform boundary between the North American plate and the Pacific plate. Transform motion also occurs at divergent boundaries. Short segments of mid-ocean ridges are connected by transform faults called fracture zones.

Why Plates Move

Scientists have proposed three mechanisms to explain how tectonic plates move over Earth's surface. Mantle convection drags plates along as mantle material moves beneath tectonic plates. Ridge push moves plates away from mid-ocean ridges as rock cools and becomes denser. Slab pull tugs plates along as the dense edge of a plate sinks beneath Earth's surface.

As atoms in Earth's core and mantle undergo radioactive decay, energy is released as heat. Some parts of the mantle become hotter than other parts. The hot parts rise as the sinking of cooler, denser material pushes the heated material up. This kind of movement of material due to differences in density is called **convection**. It was thought that as the mantle convects, or moves, it would drag the overlying tectonic plates along with it. However, many scientists have criticized this hypothesis because it does not explain the huge amount of force that would be needed to move plates.

Newly formed rock at a mid-ocean ridge is warm and less dense than older, adjacent rock. Because of its lower density, the new rock rests at a higher elevation than the older rock. The older rock slopes downward away from the ridge. As the newer, warmer rock cools, it also becomes denser. These cooling and increasingly dense rocks respond to gravity by moving down the slope of the asthenosphere, away from the ridge. This force, called **ridge push**, pushes the rest of the plate away from the mid-ocean ridge.

At subduction zones, a denser tectonic plate sinks, or subducts, beneath another, less dense plate. The leading edge of the subducting plate is colder and denser than the mantle. As it sinks, the leading edge of the plate pulls the rest of the plate with it. This process is called **slab pull**. In general, subducting plates move faster than other plates do. This evidence leads many scientists to think that slab pull may be the most important mechanism driving tectonic plate motion.

Mountains and Volcanoes

The movement of energy as heat and material in Earth's interior contribute to tectonic plate motions that result in mountain building. Mountains can form through folding, volcanism, and faulting.

Folded mountains form when rock layers are squeezed together and pushed upward. They usually form at convergent boundaries, where plates collide. For example, the Appalachian Mountains formed from folding and faulting when the North American plate collided with the Eurasian and African plates millions of years ago.

Fault-block mountains form when tension makes the lithosphere break into many normal faults. Along the faults, pieces of the lithosphere drop down compared with other pieces. The pieces left standing form fault-block mountains.

Volcanic mountains form when melted rock erupts onto Earth's surface. Many major volcanic mountains are located at convergent boundaries. Volcanic mountains can form on land or on the ocean floor. Volcanoes on the ocean floor can grow so tall that they rise above the surface of the ocean, forming islands. Most of Earth's active volcanoes are concentrated around the edge of the Pacific Ocean. This area is known as the Ring of Fire.

Volcanic eruptions also occur when an oceanic plate sinks under a continental plate. The eruptions build up mountain ranges on the continental plate, near the plate boundary. If two continental plates converge, neither plate sinks, but instead they push against each other, causing Earth's surface to push up and form mountain ranges.

Earthquakes

Earthquakes are another kind of rapid change that occurs on Earth's surface. When two plates are moving apart, Earth's outer layer is stretched and tension breaks the crust, forming large cracks called faults. This motion breaks and bends rock. Rock can become stuck as the plates scrape along. When the rocks that are stuck break free, energy is released. This makes Earth's surface shake. It causes an earthquake to occur.

Earthquakes can occur at all plate boundaries. Fault-block mountains and valleys form as plate motion causes rock to move up or down on either side of a fault. Volcanism also occurs at these boundaries as rock melts below the thinning surface. This can form volcanic mountains.

Student-Response Activity

1 Describe each of Earth's layers.

crust _____

mantle _____

core _____

2 How can this apple be compared to Earth's layers?

_____

_____

_____

_____

3 Fill in the Venn diagram to compare and contrast Earth's crust and core.

Crust

Both

Core

4 How are Earth's mantle and core different from each other?

_____

_____

_____

Benchmark Assessment SC.7.E.6.1, SC.7.E.6.5, SC.7.E.6.7

Fill in the letter of the best choice.

❶ Which is the outermost, rigid physical layer of Earth?

(A) asthenosphere

(B) inner core

(C) lithosphere

(D) outer core

❷ Which describes how scientists learn more about Earth's mantle?

(F) by studying earthquakes

(G) by studying rock that has risen due to convection

(H) by taking pictures from outside the Earth

(I) by using radioactive dating

❸ What are tectonic plate boundaries?

(A) areas where Earth's core experiences a high amount of stress

(B) areas where Earth's core experiences a low amount of stress

(C) areas where Earth's crust experiences a high amount of stress

(D) areas where Earth's mantle experiences a high amount of stress

❹ Which describes the innermost layer of Earth?

(F) It is likely made up of the metals nickel and iron.

(G) It is made up of fast moving rock.

(H) It is made up of slow moving rock.

(I) It likely has a very high concentration of oxygen.

❺ Use this diagram to answer this question.

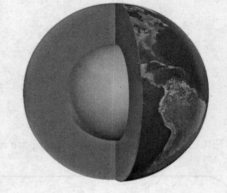

Which model of Earth's interior does this image show?

(A) the model of Earth's layers based on chemical composition

(B) the model of Earth's layers based on physical properties

(C) the model of Earth's layers based on size

(D) the model of Earth's layers based on temperature

SC.7.E.6.2 Identify the patterns within the rock cycle and relate them to surface events (weathering and erosion) and sub-surface events (plate tectonics and mountain building). **SC.7.E.6.6** Identify the impact that humans have on Earth, such as deforestation, urbanization, desertification, erosion, air and water quality, and changing the flow of water.

The Rock Cycle and Human Impact on Earth

Earth's Rocky Surface

Earth's solid parts are mostly made of rock. This rock is constantly changing and cycling through Earth. These changes cause Earth to look very differently over time.

Changing Rock

There are many processes that change rock on Earth's surface. When rock is broken down by wind, water, ice, and temperature changes, weathering occurs. When rock is weathered, it breaks down into small pieces called sediment. Water, wind, ice, and gravity can carry this sediment from one place to another through the process of erosion. When this sediment is left in one place after it has been carried, this is called deposition.

Rock can also be changed by temperature and pressure. Rocks and other materials exert pressure on the rock below it. The deeper a rock is under Earth's surface, the more pressure that is exerted on the rock. Very high temperatures can also change and melt rock.

The Rock Cycle

There are three main types of rock that exist on Earth. Igneous rock forms when magma or lava cools and hardens into a solid. Sedimentary rock forms when pieces of sediment are cemented together. Metamorphic rock is formed by pressure and temperature changes that cause rocks to undergo chemical changes.

The Rock Cycle

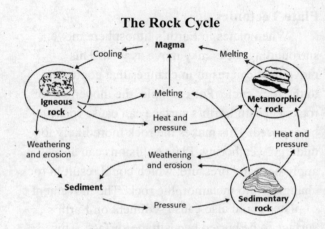

Over millions of years, rocks can change from one form to another. The series of processes that change rock in this way is called the **rock cycle**. When igneous rock is on Earth's surface, weathering can break it down into sediment. When deep below Earth's surface, high temperatures and pressure may change igneous rock into metamorphic rock. Hot temperatures can also melt igneous rock. When the melted rock cools and hardens again, it forms a new igneous rock.

As with igneous rock, high temperatures and pressure can turn sedimentary rock into metamorphic rock. High temperatures alone can melt sedimentary rock and turn it into igneous rock when it cools and hardens. If sedimentary rock is further broken down into sediments, new sedimentary rock is formed as it cements.

Metamorphic rock will change into new metamorphic rock when exposed to heat and pressure. It can also form sedimentary rock when weathered into pieces of sediment that are then cemented together. When metamorphic rock is melted, it forms igneous rock when it cools and hardens.

Plate Tectonics

When plates in Earth's lithosphere move, surrounding rocks may move as well. This movement can result in changes that contribute to the rock cycle. For example, the movement of rocks beneath Earth's surface can cause rocks to be exposed. This makes the rock more likely to undergo weathering. Plate collisions can also apply heat and pressure, which could result in rock changing into metamorphic rock. The movement of plates could also cause sediment on Earth's surface to be buried beneath the surface. This would expose rocks to higher temperatures and pressures and potentially result in the formation of igneous and metamorphic rocks.

Human Impacts on Earth

We live on land in urban or rural areas. Cities and towns are urban areas. Rural areas are open lands that may be used for farming. Humans use land in many ways. We use natural areas for recreation. We use roads that are built on land for transport. We grow crops and raise livestock on agricultural land. We live in residential areas. We build commercial businesses on land and extract resources such as metals and water from the land.

Human activities can have positive and negative effects on land and soil. Some activities restore land to its natural state, or increase the amount of fertile soil on land. Other activities can degrade land. Land degradation is the process by which human activity and natural processes damage land to the point that it can no longer support the local ecosystem. Urbanization, deforestation, and poor farming practices can all lead to land degradation.

Deforestation

The removal of trees and other vegetation from an area is called **deforestation**. Logging for wood can cause deforestation. Surface mining causes deforestation by removing vegetation and soil to get to the minerals below. Deforestation also occurs in rain forests when farmers cut or burn down trees so they can grow crops. Deforestation leads to increased soil erosion.

Urbanization

Rural areas have large areas of open land and low densities of people. Urban areas have dense human populations and small areas of open land. This means that more people live in a square km of an urban area than live in a square km of a rural area. **Urbanization** is the growth of urban areas caused by people moving into cities. When cities increase in size, the population of rural areas near the city may decrease. When an area becomes urbanized, buildings, parking lots, and roads replace its natural land surface. City parks, which contain natural surfaces, may also be built in urban areas. Urbanization can cause deforestation when forests are replaced with buildings.

Desertification

When too many livestock are kept in one area, they can overgraze the area. Overgrazing removes the plants and roots that hold topsoil together. Overgrazing and other poor farming methods can cause desertification. **Desertification** is the process by which land becomes more desert-like and unable to support life. Without plants, soil becomes dusty and prone to wind erosion. Deforestation and urbanization can also lead to desertification.

Erosion

Erosion is the process by which wind, water, or gravity transports soil and sediment from one place to another. Some type of erosion occurs on most land. However, erosion can speed up when land is degraded. Roots of trees and plants act as anchors to the soil. When land is cleared for farming, the trees and plants are removed, and the soil is no longer protected. This exposes soil to blowing wind and running water that can wash away the soil.

Air and Water Quality

The contamination of the atmosphere by pollutants from human and natural sources is called air pollution. Natural sources of air pollution include volcanic eruptions, wildfires, and dust storms. In cities and suburbs, most air pollution comes from the burning of fossil fuels such as oil, gasoline, and coal. Oil refineries, chemical manufacturing plants, dry-cleaning businesses, and auto-repair shops are just some potential sources of air pollution. Scientists classify air pollutants as either gases or particulates.

When waste or other material is added to water so that it is harmful to organisms that use it or live in it, water pollution occurs. It is useful to divide pollution sources into two types. Point-source pollution comes from one specific site. For example, a major chemical spill is point-source pollution. Usually this type of pollution can be controlled once its source is found. Nonpoint-source pollution comes from many small sources and is more difficult to control. Most nonpoint-source pollution reaches water supplies by runoff or by seeping into groundwater. The main sources of nonpoint-source pollution are city streets, roads and drains, farms, and mines.

Changing the Flow of Water

Pumping and collecting groundwater and surface waters changes how water flows in natural systems. For example, a reservoir is a body of water that usually forms behind a dam. Dams stop river waters from flowing along their natural course. The water in a reservoir would naturally have flowed to the sea. Instead, the water can be diverted into a pipeline or into artificial channels called canals or aqueducts.

Student-Response Activity

 Describe the role that weathering and erosion play in the rock cycle.

_____

_____

_____

_____

_____

❷ Label the missing parts of the diagram.

❸ Compare and contrast how sedimentary and metamorphic rocks form.

_____
_____
_____
_____
_____
_____

❹ What are three ways humans impact the Earth? Explain your reasoning.

_____
_____
_____
_____
_____
_____
_____
_____

Benchmark Assessment SC.7.E.6.2, SC.7.E.6.6

Fill in the letter of the best choice.

❶ These rock formations in Turkey are known as the fairy chimneys. Which natural process **most likely** shaped these rocks?

- Ⓐ deposition
- Ⓑ erosion
- Ⓒ temperature and pressure
- Ⓓ weathering

❷ Which **best** describes deposition?

- Ⓕ It is the process by which rocks change from one form to another.
- Ⓖ It is the process by which sediment comes to rest.
- Ⓗ It is the process by which sediment is moved from one place to another.
- Ⓘ It is the process by which water, wind, ice and temperature changes break down rock.

❸ Which ways can plate-tectonic motion cause changes in rock?

- Ⓐ It can expose rock beneath Earth's surface to wind and water.
- Ⓑ It can expose rock to energy from the sun, which breaks rock down.
- Ⓒ The movement of plates changes sediments into igneous rock.
- Ⓓ The shaking of plates causes rock to undergo chemical reactions.

❹ What can result from deforestation by humans?

- Ⓕ better water quality
- Ⓖ desertification
- Ⓗ less erosion
- Ⓘ less urbanization

❺ Which describes how igneous rock forms?

- Ⓐ Magma or lava cools and hardens into a solid.
- Ⓑ Pieces of sediment are broken down.
- Ⓒ Pieces of sediment are cemented together.
- Ⓓ Pressure and temperature changes cause chemical changes.

SC.7.E.6.3 Identify current methods for measuring the age of Earth and its parts, including the law of superposition and radioactive dating. **SC.7.E.6.4** Explain and give examples of how physical evidence supports scientific theories that Earth has evolved over geologic time due to natural processes.

Earth's History

Earth's Age

Scientists use many different clues and tools to determine the age of the Earth. Absolute and relative dating are two techniques used to determine the age of Earth and the rocks on its surface.

Superposition in Rock Layers

When scientists examine layers of undisturbed rock, they know that the layers on the bottom were formed first. This means that these layers are older. The layers on top were likely formed last, which means that those layers are younger. This principle is called superposition. If left undisturbed, the sediment will remain in horizontal layers.

Superposition can be seen in many different situations. If you stack a pile of newspapers one at a time, on top of one another, the newspapers that you place first will sit on the bottom. This is generally true unless the newspapers are knocked down or disturbed in some other way. The same is true for layers of rock.

One way rock layers and the principle of superposition can be disturbed is by tilting. This happens when Earth's forces move rock layers up or down unevenly. The layers become slanted. Folding can also disturb rock layers. This happens when rock layers are squeezed together. It can cause the layers to be turned over so much that older layers end up on top of younger layers.

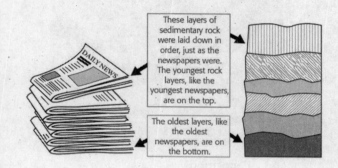

These layers of sedimentary rock were laid down in order, just as the newspapers were. The youngest rock layers, like the youngest newspapers, are on the top.

The oldest layers, like the oldest newspapers, are on the bottom.

Relative Dating

The principle of superposition allows scientists to compare the age of one rock or fossil to another. This is called **relative dating**. While relative dating can tell scientists whether something is older or younger, it cannot tell scientists exactly how old something is.

Absolute Dating

Absolute dating is determining the actual age of an event or object. One way that scientists determine the absolute ages of rocks is using radioactive isotopes. Isotopes are atoms of the same element that have a different number of neutrons. Some isotopes are stable while others are unstable. The unstable isotopes are called radioactive. When these radioactive isotopes decay, their decay happens at a constant rate and are measured in half-lives. A half-life is the time needed for half a sample of a radioactive isotope to undergo decay.

Since scientists know how fast a radioactive isotope decays, they can figure out a rock's absolute age. To do this, they analyze the percentages of radioactive isotope and daughter isotope (the isotopes left over after the decay) in the rock sample. For example, if a sample of rock contains a radioactive isotope that has a half-life of 4 million years, and there are equal amounts of parent and daughter isotopes, it can be determined that 1 half-life has passed. Since the radioactive isotope has a half-life of 4 million years, it can be determined that 4 million years has passed. This method of dating rock is called **radiometric dating**. There are different methods of radiometric dating that are used for different substances.

Radiometric dating of rock can be used to determine the age of Earth. Since rocks that were formed with the formation of Earth have been eroded, melted, or buried, scientists cannot use those rocks to determine Earth's age. Instead, meteorites, rocks from the surface of the moon, and rocks from various places in our solar system are used. When radiometric dating is done on those rocks, they show that Earth is about 4.6 billion years old.

Evolution of Earth over Geologic Time

As new layers of sediment are deposited, they cover older layers. Older layers become compacted. Dissolved minerals, such as calcite and quartz separate from water that passes through the sediment. Scientists use different characteristics to classify sedimentary rock. These provide evidence of the environment that the sedimentary rock once formed in. It shows how the Earth once was, even if it has since changed.

Mud cracks, for example, form when fine-grained sediments at the bottom of a shallow body of water are exposed to the air and dry out. Mud cracks show that an ancient lake, stream, or ocean shoreline was once a part of an area.

Mud Cracks

Ripple marks also show the motion of wind or water waves over sediment. Ice cores, also give a history of Earth's climate over time. Some ice cores have regular layers, called bands, which form each year. Band size shows how much precipitation fell during a given time. The composition of water and concentration of gases in the ice core show the conditions of the atmosphere at the time that the ice formed.

Name ______________________ Date __________

Benchmark Review
SC.7.E.6.3, SC.7.E.6.4

Student-Response Activity

1. Explain why rocks from Earth cannot be used to determine Earth's age.

2. Give an example of how both relative dating and absolute dating could be used together to date igneous and sedimentary rocks that are found together.

3. What layout are rock layers supposed to be in according to the principle of superposition and how can this layout be disturbed?

4. What are two physical examples of how Earth has evolved over time?

Benchmark Assessment SC.7.E.6.3, SC.7.E.6.4

Fill in the letter of the best choice.

1 Which does **not** show Earth's past environment?
(A) ice cores
(B) mud cracks
(C) ripple marks
(D) rock color

2 What do scientists do to find the absolute age of rocks?
(F) They analyze the layout of rock layers.
(G) They analyze the percentage of only radioactive isotopes.
(H) They analyze the percentages of radioactive isotope and daughter isotope.
(I) They count the number of rock layers.

3 Which example **best** represents superposition?
(A) a layered cake
(B) a pile of toys
(C) pens in a jar
(D) people standing in a group

4 Which is a drawback of relative dating?
(F) It does not tell you the exact age of something.
(G) It is very time consuming to do.
(H) It rarely can be done successfully.
(I) It requires a large amount of resources.

5 Which describes the principle of superposition?
(A) All the rock layers are the same age.
(B) Older rock layers are at the bottom, and younger layers are at the top.
(C) The rock layers alternate every other layer between younger and older.
(D) Younger rock layers are at the bottom and older layers are at the top.

SC.6.E.7.1 Differentiate among radiation, conduction, and convection, the three mechanisms by which heat is transferred through Earth's system. **SC.6.E.7.5** Explain how energy provided by the Sun influences global patterns of atmospheric movement and the temperature differences between air, water, and land.

Heat Transfer

Heat

Heat is a type of energy that causes objects to feel hot or cold. It can be transferred between objects at different temperatures. The direction of heat transfer is always from the object with the higher temperature to the object with the lower temperature. This means that when you touch something hot, heat transfers from the object to your body.

Heat Transfer

When the same amount of energy is transferred, some materials will get warmer or cooler at a rate that is faster than other materials. Suppose you are walking on the beach on a sunny day. You may notice the land feels warmer than the air and the water, even though they are exposed to the same amount of energy from the sun. This is because the land warms up at a faster rate than the water and air do. Heat energy is transferred in three ways: radiation, convection, and conduction.

Energy Transfer by Radiation

On a summer day, you can feel warmth from the sun on your skin. How did that energy reach you from the sun? The sun transfers energy to Earth by radiation. **Radiation** is the transfer of energy as electromagnetic waves. Radiation can transfer energy between objects that are not in direct contact with each other. Many objects other than the sun also radiate energy as light and heat. These include a hot burner on a stove and a campfire.

The sun also heats land. Radiation from the sun hits land and transfers energy, causing the ground to warm. Water and air can move freely but land cannot. Even so, thermal energy stored in the ground can also be transferred. Some energy is released from the ground as radiation. Have you ever felt heat rising from the ground after a sunny day? If so, you have felt radiation.

Have you ever watched a pot of boiling water? If so, you have seen convection.

Convection is the transfer of energy due to the movement of matter. As water warms up at the bottom of the pot, some of the hot water rises. At the same time, cooler water from other parts of the pot sink and replace the rising water. This water is then warmed and the cycle continues. While convection usually happens in fluids, it can happen in solids as well. Matter—the water—has transferred heat energy due to its movement.

Convection involves the movement of matter due to differences in density. As most matter gets warmer, it undergoes thermal expansion as well as a decrease in its density. The less-dense matter gets forced upward by the surrounding colder, denser matter that sinks. As the hot matter rises, it cools and becomes denser, causing it to sink back down. This cycling of matter is called a **convection current**.

Convection takes place most often in fluids, such as water and air. If Earth's surface is warmer than the air, energy will be transferred from the ground to the air. As the air becomes warmer, it becomes less dense. This air is pushed upward and out of the way by cooler, denser air that is sinking. As the warm air rises, it cools and becomes denser and begins to sink back toward Earth's surface. This cycle moves energy through the atmosphere.

Convection currents also occur in the ocean because of differences in the density of ocean water. More-dense water sinks to the ocean floor, and less-dense water moves toward the surface. Temperature and the amount of salt in the water both affect the density of ocean water. Cold water is more dense than warm water, and water with a lot of salt is more dense than less-salty water.

Energy produced deep inside Earth heats rock in the mantle. The heated rock becomes less dense and is pushed up toward Earth's surface by the cooler, denser surrounding rock. Once cooled near the surface, the rock sinks. These convection currents transfer energy from Earth's core toward Earth's surface. These currents also cause the movement of tectonic plates.

Energy Transfer by Conduction

Have you ever touched an ice cube and wondered why it feels cold? An ice cube has only a small amount of energy, compared to your hand. Energy is transferred to the ice cube from your hand through the process of conduction. **Conduction** is the transfer of energy from one object to another object through direct contact. Even a solid block of ice has particles in constant motion.

Conduction involves the faster-moving particles of the warmer object transferring energy to the slower-moving particles in the cooler object. When objects of different temperatures touch, the moving particles in both objects interact. The warmer object has faster moving particles that have more kinetic energy. These particles transfer some of their energy to the object with the slower moving particles and less energy. For example, conduction happens when you place your hand on a warm object. Heat from the object warms your hand as its particles transfer energy to the particles in your hand.

Conduction allows energy to move among land, the atmosphere, and the ocean. Interactions between the ocean and the atmosphere drive global weather patterns.

Energy can be transferred between the geosphere and the atmosphere by conduction. When cooler air molecules come into direct contact with the warm ground, energy is passed to the air by conduction. Conduction between the ground and the air happens only within a few centimeters of Earth's surface.

Conduction also takes place between air particles and water particles. For example, if air transfers enough energy to liquid water, the water may evaporate. If water vapor transfers energy to the air, the kinetic energy of the water decreases. As a result, the water vapor may condense to form liquid water droplets.

Energy transfers by conduction between rock particles inside Earth. However, rock is a poor conductor of heat, so this process happens very slowly.

Wind

The next time you feel the wind blowing, you can thank the sun! The sun does not warm the whole surface of the Earth in a uniform manner. This uneven heating causes the air above Earth's surface to be at different temperatures. Cold air is more dense than warm air, which causes the cold air to sink. When the colder, more dense air sinks, it places greater pressure on the surface of Earth than warmer, less-dense air does. This results in areas of higher air pressure. Air moves from areas of higher pressure toward areas of lower pressure. The movement of air caused by differences in air pressure is called wind. The greater the differences in air pressure, the faster the air moves.

Cold, dense air at the poles causes areas of high pressure to form at the poles. Warm, less-dense air at the equator forms an area of lower pressure. This pressure gradient results in global movement of air. However, instead of moving in one circle between the equator and the poles, air moves in smaller circular patterns called **convection cells**. As air moves from the equator, it cools and becomes denser. At about 30°N latitude and 30°S latitude, a high-pressure belt results from the sinking of air. Near the poles, cold air warms as it moves away from the poles. At around 60°N latitude and 60°S latitude, a low-pressure belt forms as the warmed air is pushed upward.

Student-Response Activity

1   What is an example of conduction on Earth? Explain your answer.

_____

_____

_____

_____

2   This image shows the location of convection at different latitudes around the globe.
Explain what causes convection to take place.

_____

_____

_____

_____

_____

3   What is the main source of energy for most processes at Earth's surface?

_____

_____

4   What happens when two objects at different temperatures touch? Name one place where
it occurs on Earth.

_____

_____

_____

_____

Benchmark Assessment SC.6.E.7.1 and SC.6.E.7.5

Fill in the letter of the best choice.

1 When energy from the sun hits the air above land, the air warms up and rises. Along a coastline, cooler air above the ocean flows toward the land and replaces this rising air. Which **best** describes these processes?

(A) conduction and convection

(B) conduction, convection, and radiation

(C) radiation and conduction

(D) radiation and convection

2 In order for heat to transfer from one object to another, which must be **true**?

(F) The objects must be different sizes.

(G) The objects must be different temperatures.

(H) The objects must be the same size.

(I) The objects must be the same temperature.

3 Which describes what happens when cooler air particles come into contact with the warmer ground?

(A) The particles do not interact.

(B) Energy is transferred from the cooler air to the warmer ground.

(C) Energy is transferred from the warmer ground to the cooler air.

(D) The particles move back and forth between the air and the ground.

Use the image to answer Questions 4–6.

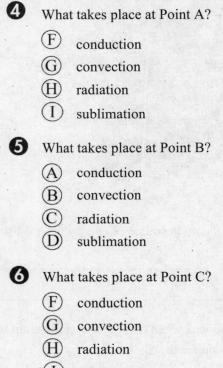

4 What takes place at Point A?

(F) conduction

(G) convection

(H) radiation

(I) sublimation

5 What takes place at Point B?

(A) conduction

(B) convection

(C) radiation

(D) sublimation

6 What takes place at Point C?

(F) conduction

(G) convection

(H) radiation

(I) sublimation

SC.6.E.7.4 Differentiate and show interactions among the geosphere, hydrosphere, cryosphere, atmosphere, and biosphere. SC.6.E.7.6 Differentiate between weather and climate. SC.6.E.7.9 Describe how the composition and structure of the atmosphere protects life and insulates the planet.

The Atmosphere and Biosphere

What Are Earth's Systems?

A system is a group of related objects or parts that work together to form a whole. From the center of the planet to the outer edge of the atmosphere, Earth is a system. The Earth system is all of the matter, energy, and processes within Earth's boundary. Earth is a complex system made up of many smaller systems. The Earth system is made of nonliving things, such as rocks, air, and water. It also contains living things, such as trees, animals, and people.

Matter and energy continuously cycle through the smaller systems that make up the Earth system. The Earth system can be divided into five main parts—the geosphere, the hydrosphere, the cryosphere, the atmosphere, and the biosphere.

The Five Main Systems

The **geosphere** is the mostly solid, rocky part of Earth. It extends from the center of Earth to the outer layer. The core, mantle, and crust make up the geosphere. The crust is the thin, outermost layer of the geosphere. The crust is divided into plates that move slowly over Earth's surface. The crust beneath the oceans is called oceanic crust, and is only 5 to 10 km thick. The continents are made of continental crust, and they range in thickness from about 15 to 70 km. Continental crust is thickest beneath mountain ranges. The crust is made mostly of silicate minerals.

The mantle lies just below the crust. A small layer of the solid mantle, right below the crust, is just soft enough to flow. Movements in this layer move the plates of the crust. The mantle is about 2,900 km thick. It is made of silicate minerals that are denser than those in the crust.

The central part of Earth is the core, which has a radius of 3,500 km. It is made of iron and nickel and is very dense.

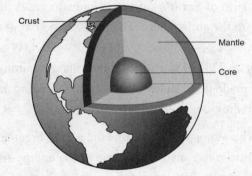

The **hydrosphere** is the part of Earth that is liquid water. Ninety-seven percent of all water on Earth is the salt water found in the oceans. Oceans cover 71% of Earth's surface. The hydrosphere also includes the water in lakes, rivers, and marshes. Clouds and rain are also parts of the hydrosphere. Even water that is underground is part of the hydrosphere. The water on Earth is constantly moving. It moves through the ocean in currents, because of wind and differences in the density of ocean waters. Water also moves from Earth's surface to the air by evaporation. It falls back to Earth as rain. It flows in rivers and through rocks under the ground. It even moves into and out of living things.

Earth's **cryosphere** is made up of all of the frozen water on Earth. Therefore, all of the snow, ice, sea ice, glaciers, ice shelves, icebergs, and frozen ground are a part of the cryosphere. Most of the frozen water on Earth is found in the ice caps in Antarctica and in the Arctic. However, snow and glaciers are found in the mountains and at high altitudes all over the world. The amount of frozen water in most of these areas often changes with the seasons. These changes, in turn, play an important role in Earth's climate and in the survival of many species.

The **atmosphere** is a mixture of mostly invisible gases that surrounds Earth. The atmosphere extends outward about 500 to 600 km from the surface of Earth. But most of the gases lie within 8 to 50 km of Earth's surface. The main gases that make up the atmosphere are nitrogen and oxygen. About 78% of the atmosphere is nitrogen. Oxygen makes up 21% of the atmosphere. The remaining 1% is made up of many other gases, including argon, carbon dioxide, and water vapor.

The atmosphere contains the air we breathe. The atmosphere also traps some of the energy from the sun's rays. This energy helps keep Earth warm enough for living things to survive and multiply. Uneven warming by the sun gives rise to winds and air currents that move large amounts of air around the world.

The atmosphere surrounds and protects Earth. It also protects Earth from harmful solar radiation and from space debris that enters the Earth system. The ozone layer is an area in the stratosphere, 15 km to 40 km above Earth's surface, where ozone is highly concentrated. The ozone layer absorbs most of the solar radiation.

The atmosphere also controls the temperature on Earth. Without the atmosphere, Earth's average temperature would be very low. The greenhouse effect is the process by which gases in the atmosphere, such as water vapor and carbon dioxide, absorb and give off infrared radiation. Radiation from the sun warms Earth's surface, and Earth's surface gives off infrared radiation.

The **biosphere** is made up of living things and the areas of Earth where they are found. The rocks, soil, oceans, lakes, rivers, and lower atmosphere all support life. Organisms have even been found deep in Earth's crust and high in clouds. But no matter where they live, all organisms need certain factors to survive. Many organisms need oxygen or carbon dioxide to carry out life processes. Liquid water is also important for most living things. Many organisms also need moderate temperatures. You will not find a polar bear living in a desert because it is too hot for the polar bear. However, some organisms do live in extreme environments, such as in ice at the poles and at volcanic vents on the sea floor. A stable source of energy is also important for life. For example, plants and algae use the energy from sunlight to make their food. Other organisms get their energy by eating these plants or algae.

Interactions Among Earth's Systems

Earth's spheres interact as matter and energy change and cycle among the five different spheres. These interactions make life on Earth possible. Remember that the Earth system includes all the matter, energy, and processes within Earth's boundary.

If matter or energy never changed from one form to another, life on Earth would not be possible. Imagine what would happen if there were no more rain and all fresh water drained into the oceans. Most of the life on land would quickly die. But how do these different spheres interact? An example of an interaction is when water cycles among land, ocean, air, and living things. To move between and among these different spheres, water absorbs, releases, and transports energy all over the world in its different forms.

Matter and Energy Exchanged Among Spheres

Earth's spheres interact as matter moves between and among spheres. For example, the atmosphere interacts with the hydrosphere or cryosphere when rain or snow falls from the air. The opposite also happens as water from the hydrosphere and cryosphere moves into the atmosphere. Sometimes, matter moves through different spheres. For example, some bacteria in the biosphere remove nitrogen gas from the atmosphere. These bacteria then release a different form of nitrogen into the soil, or geosphere. Plants in the biosphere use this nitrogen to grow. When the plant dies and decays, the nitrogen is released in different forms. One of these forms returns to the atmosphere.

Earth's spheres also interact as energy moves between them. For example, plants use solar energy to make their food. Some of this energy is passed on to animals that eat plants. Some of the energy is released into the atmosphere as heat as the animals move around. Some of the energy is released into the geosphere when organisms die and decay. In this case, energy enters the biosphere and moves into the atmosphere and geosphere.

Energy also moves back and forth between spheres. For example, solar energy reflected by Earth's surface warms up the atmosphere, creating winds. Winds create waves and surface ocean currents that travel across the world's oceans. When warm winds and ocean currents reach colder areas, thermal energy moves into the colder air, warming it up. In this case, the energy has cycled between the atmosphere and the hydrosphere.

Weather and Climate

Weather conditions change from day to day. Weather is the condition of Earth's atmosphere at a particular time and place. Climate, on the other hand, describes the weather conditions in an area over a long period of time. For the most part, climate is determined by temperature and precipitation. But what factors affect the temperature and precipitation rates of an area? Those factors include latitude, wind patterns, elevation, locations of mountains and large bodies of water, and nearness to ocean currents.

Student-Response Activity

1 What are the five main parts of the Earth system? Provide a description for each part.

_____

_____

_____

_____

_____

2 Fill in the Venn diagram to compare the hydrosphere and the cryosphere.

Hydrosphere

Both

Cryosphere

3 What would happen to life on Earth if the ozone layer were not present?

_____

_____

_____

4 Use the diagram to list examples of things that make up the biosphere, hydrosphere, and geosphere.

_____

_____

_____

_____

Benchmark Assessment SC.6.E.7.4, SC.6.E.7.6, SC.6.E.7.9

Fill in the letter of the best choice.

For Questions 1 and 2, use the graph showing the composition of Earth's atmosphere. Each part represents a type of gas.

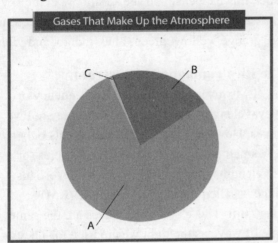

Gases That Make Up the Atmosphere

❶ Which gas is represented by part A on the graph?

(A) carbon dioxide

(B) nitrogen

(C) oxygen

(D) water vapor

❷ Which gas is represented by part B on the graph?

(F) carbon dioxide

(G) nitrogen

(H) oxygen

(I) water vapor

❸ Which is an example of the cycling of matter from one sphere to another?

(A) a puddle of water evaporating and rising into the atmosphere

(B) animals obtaining energy from plants

(C) heat energy from the sun warming the land

(D) heat energy from the sun warming the oceans

❹ When heat moves from the ocean to the surrounding air, which is this an example of?

(F) the transfer of energy from the atmosphere to the hydrosphere

(G) the transfer of energy from the hydrosphere to the atmosphere

(H) the transfer of matter from the atmosphere to the hydrosphere

(I) the transfer of matter from the hydrosphere to the atmosphere

❺ Which system includes all life on Earth?

(A) biosphere

(B) cryosphere

(C) geosphere

(D) hydrosphere

SC.7.P.10.1 Illustrate that the sun's energy arrives as radiation with a wide range of wavelengths, including infrared, visible, and ultraviolet, and that white light is made up of a spectrum of many different colors.

The Electromagnetic Spectrum

Radiation from the Sun

Light is a type of energy that travels as a wave, but light is different from other types of waves. Light waves are vibrating electric and magnetic fields moving through space that transfer energy. When an electrically charged particle vibrates, its fields also vibrate, producing an electromagnetic (EM) wave. This vibration carries energy released by the original vibration of the particle. Radiation is energy that has been transmitted by waves or particles, so this transfer of energy is called EM radiation.

Most electromagnetic waves Earth receives from the sun are infrared light, ultraviolet light, and visible light. When you are out in the sun and feel warm, you feel infrared light from the sun as heat. You might wear sunglasses outside to protect your eyes from ultraviolet light. Too much exposure to ultraviolet light can damage cells.

The Color of Light

Light comes in many colors, from red to violet. Like all waves, light has wavelengths. Our eyes interpret different wavelengths of light as different colors. The shortest wavelengths are seen as violet, and the longest ones are seen as red. Even the longest wavelengths we can see are still very small—less than one ten-thousandth of a centimeter.

We perceive white light when we see all the wavelengths of light at once, in equal proportions. A prism can split white light into its component colors, separating the colors by wavelength. When it rains, drops of water act like tiny prisms, splitting white light into various wavelengths.

When this happens, you see a rainbow in the sky consisting of all the colors of the visible spectrum: red, orange, yellow, green, blue, indigo, and violet.

The Electromagnetic Spectrum

EM waves are measured by frequency or by wavelength. The light waves we see are EM waves. However, visible light represents only a very small part of the range of frequencies (or wavelengths) that an EM wave can have. This range is called the **electromagnetic (EM) spectrum**. These other EM waves are the same type of wave as the light we are used to. They are just different frequencies. Two parts of the spectrum are close to visible light. **Infrared**, or IR, light has slightly longer wavelengths than red light. **Ultraviolet**, or UV, light has slightly shorter wavelengths than violet light.

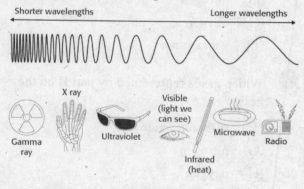

People use forms of light across the electromagnetic spectrum for different functions. Satellites in space can detect electromagnetic radiation from objects and use this to create images. When you listen to the radio, radio waves are transmitting the sound you hear. Radio waves have the longest wavelengths. They are used to broadcast many signals, including radio, television, and alarm systems. Microwaves, which are not the shortest EM waves, heat food quickly and are used in cellular phones. We feel infrared light as heat. Infrared imaging can locate objects that emit heat by creating a thermogram, which is a visual representation of temperature.

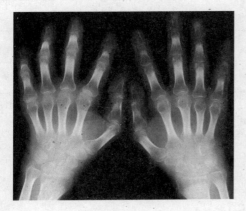

Doctors can use ultraviolet light to sterilize medical equipment, x-rays to make images of a person's bones, and gamma rays to treat some forms of cancer.

Radiation from the Sun

Between the sun and us lies Earth's atmosphere. In order to see anything, some of the sun's light must make it through the atmosphere. However, not all wavelengths of light penetrate the atmosphere equally. The atmosphere blocks most of the higher-frequency radiation, such as x-rays and gamma rays, from reaching us at the ground level, while allowing most of the visible light to reach us.

There is a "window" of radio frequencies that are barely blocked at all. Radio and visible light penetrate all the way to the ground. Most ultraviolet light is blocked high in the atmosphere.

The atmosphere blocks much of the sun's radiation, but not all. Some EM radiation can be dangerous to humans, so we take extra steps to protect ourselves. Receiving too much ultraviolet (UV) radiation can cause sunburn, skin cancer, or damage to the eyes, so we wear sunscreen and wear UV-blocking sunglasses to protect us from the UV light that passes through the atmosphere. You need this protection even on overcast days because UV light can travel through clouds.

Outer space is often thought of as being cold, but despite this, one of the biggest dangers to astronauts is from overheating! Outside of Earth's protective atmosphere, the level of dangerous EM radiation is much higher. Also, in the vacuum of space, it is much harder to dispose of any unwanted energy, because there is no surrounding matter (such as air) to absorb the extra energy. Astronauts need extra protection from EM radiation in space. This is why astronauts' helmets are made to be highly reflective, using a thin layer of pure gold to reflect back unwanted EM radiation.

Student-Response Activity

❶ List, in order from longest to shortest wavelength, the different colors of the visible portion of the EM spectrum.

_____

_____

_____

_____

❷ What type of EM waves do doctors use to take a picture of your bones?

_____

_____

❸ Complete the Venn diagram to compare and contrast radio waves and infrared radiation.

Radio waves

Both

Infrared

❹ When you go outside and wear sunglasses, what type of radiation are you protecting your eyes from?

_____

_____

❺ Why do astronauts need to be concerned about EM waves in outer space?

_____

_____

_____

Benchmark Assessment SC.7.P.10.1

Fill in the letter of the best choice.

❶ Which type of electromagnetic radiation has the shortest wavelength?

(A) microwaves

(B) radio waves

(C) ultraviolet light

(D) visible light

❷ What happens to frequency as wavelength increases across the electromagnetic spectrum?

(F) Frequency and wavelength are not related.

(G) Frequency decreases.

(H) Frequency increases.

(I) Frequency stays the same.

❸ Which type of EM radiation is felt as heat?

(A) infrared

(B) microwaves

(C) radio waves

(D) ultraviolet

❹ Examine the image shown below.

What can you infer about the radiation in the right side of this spectrum?

(F) The radiation has a very high frequency compared to other radiation.

(G) The radiation is not emitted by the sun.

(H) The radiation is used to transmit sound.

(I) The radiation is visible.

❺ Which statement is **not** true about light?

(A) All types of light waves have the same wavelength.

(B) Light waves are vibrating electric and magnetic fields.

(C) Light waves can transfer energy.

(D) Visible light comes in many colors.

SC.7.P.10.2 Observe and explain that light can be reflected, refracted, and/or absorbed.
SC.7.P.10.3 Recognize that light waves, sound waves, and other waves move at different speeds in different materials.

Properties of Waves

Light Passes Through Matter

Light travels through empty space. When light encounters a material, it can be passed through the material, or transmitted. The medium can transmit all, some, or none of the light. Matter that transmits light is transparent. Air, water, and some types of glass are transparent materials. Objects can be seen clearly through transparent materials. But when light waves pass through a medium, the medium can change properties of the light.

You may have learned that light always travels at the same speed in a vacuum. However, light travels slower in a medium. Light travels a bit slower in air than in a vacuum. Light travels only about three-fourths as fast in water as in a vacuum, and only about two-thirds as fast in glass as in a vacuum. Although light of all wavelengths travels at the same speed in a vacuum, the same is not true in a medium. When light enters a medium from a vacuum, shorter wavelengths are slowed more than longer wavelengths. In a medium, the speed of violet light is less than the speed of red light.

A straight object, such as a straw, looks bent or broken when part of it is underwater. Light from the straw changes direction when it passes from water to glass and from glass to air. **Refraction** is the change in direction of a wave when it passes from one medium to another at an angle. Your brain always interprets light as traveling in a straight line. You perceive the straw where it would be if light traveled in a straight line.

The light reflected by the straw in air does travel in a straight line to your eye. But the light from the lower part of the straw changes direction when it passes into air. It refracts, causing the illusion that the bottom part of the straw in a water glass is disconnected from the top part.

Refraction is due to the change in speed as a wave enters a new medium. In glass, light's speed depends on wavelength. When light passes through a glass prism, the light waves with shorter wavelengths change direction more than waves with longer wavelengths. So, a prism separates light into a spectrum of colors.

Matter Can Absorb or Reflect Light

Opaque materials do not let any light pass through them. Instead they reflect light, absorb light, or both. Many materials, such as wood, brick, or metal, are opaque.

When light enters a material, but does not leave it, the light is absorbed. Absorption is the transfer of light energy to matter. A shirt that absorbs light appears opaque.

However, absorption is not the only way an object can be opaque.

You see an object only when light from the object enters your eye. However, most objects do not give off, or emit, light. Instead, light bounces off the object's surface. The bouncing of light off a surface is called **reflection**.

Most objects have a surface that is at least slightly rough. When light strikes a rough surface, such as wood or cloth, the light reflects in many different directions. Some of the reflected light reaches your eyes, and you see the object.

Light bounces at an angle equal to the angle at which it hit the surface. When light strikes a smooth or shiny surface such as a mirror, it reflects in a uniform way. As a result, a mirror produces an image. Light from a lamp might be reflected by your skin, then be reflected by a mirror, and then enter your eye. You look at the mirror and see yourself.

Light is Reflected or Absorbed

Visible light includes a range of colors. Light that includes all colors is called white light. When white light strikes an object, the object can transmit some or all of the colors of light, reflect some or all of the colors, and absorb some or all of the colors.

The perceived color of an object is determined by the colors of light reflected by the object. For example, a frog's skin absorbs most colors of light, but reflects most of the green light. When you look in the direction of the frog, the green light enters your eyes, so the frog appears green. An object that reflects every color appears white. An object that absorbs every color appears black.

Student-Response Activity

❶ Are the books on the table transparent or opaque? How do you know?

_____

_____

_____

_____

_____

_____

❷ Emma draws a sketch of what happens to light as it moves through air and then into a tank of water. Describe what happens to the speed of light as it enters the water.

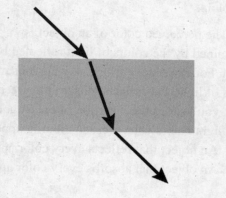

_____

_____

_____

_____

_____

❸ Paul shines light on a mirror. He draws a diagram to show what happens to the light. What behavior does the light exhibit?

Light in

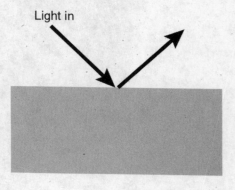

_____

_____

_____

_____

❹ Why does a frog look green?

_____

_____

_____

❺ Bernard has a black shirt. What colors of light does the material absorb?

_____

_____

_____

Benchmark Assessment SC.7.P.10.2, SC.7.P.10.3

Fill in the letter of the best choice.

❶ Which color of light bends the **most** when passing through a prism?

(A) blue
(B) green
(C) orange
(D) red

❷ What term applies to matter that light can pass through?

(F) cloudy
(G) opaque
(H) translucent
(I) transparent

❸ What is the transfer of light energy to matter called?

(A) absorption
(B) reflection
(C) refraction
(D) scattering

❹ Which statement is **true** about the speed of light?

(F) It travels fastest in air.
(G) It travels fastest in a vacuum.
(H) It travels the slowest in glass.
(I) It travels the slowest in water.

❺ A student puts a straw in a glass of water and notices that it appears bent as shown in the photo below. Which behavior is shown in the image of the straw in the glass of water?

(A) absorption
(B) reflection
(C) refraction
(D) scattering

🟦 **Benchmark Review**
SC.7.P.11.1, SC.7.P.11.4

SC.7.P.11.1 Recognize that adding heat to or removing heat from a system may result in a temperature change and possibly a change of state. **SC.7.P.11.4** Observe and describe that heat flows in predictable ways, moving from warmer objects to cooler ones until they reach the same temperature.

Temperature and Heat

Kinetic Theory of Matter

All matter is made up of atoms. These particles are always moving even if it does not look as if they are. The kinetic theory of matter states that all of the particles that make up matter are constantly in motion. Because the particles are in motion, they have kinetic energy. The faster the particles are moving, the more kinetic energy they have.

While the particles of matter are constantly moving, they move in different directions and at different speeds. This motion is random. Therefore, the individual particles of matter have different amounts of kinetic energy. The average kinetic energy of all these particles takes into account their different random movements.

The kinetic theory of matter explains the motion of particles in solids, liquids, and gases.

- The particles in a solid, such as concrete, are not free to move around very much. They vibrate back and forth in the same position and are held tightly together by forces of attraction.
- The particles in a liquid, such as water in a pool, move more freely than particles in a solid. They are constantly sliding around and tumbling over each other as they move.
- In a gas, such as the air around you, particles are far apart and move around at high speeds. Particles collide with one another, but otherwise they do not interact much.

Kinetic Energy and Temperature

Temperature is a measure of the average kinetic energy of all the particles in an object. In a colder liquid, the particles are moving slower. In a warmer liquid, the particles are moving faster. You know that the particles in a substance have a greater kinetic energy at a warmer temperature. There are three common temperature scales: Celcius, Fahrenheit, and Kelvin. All three temperature scales measure the average kinetic energy of particles. An instrument known as a thermometer is used to measure temperature.

Thermal Energy, Temperature, and Heat

Temperature and thermal energy are different from one another. Temperature is related to the average kinetic energy of the particles, while thermal energy is the total kinetic energy of all of the particles in a substance. A glass of water can have the same temperature as a lake, but the lake has more thermal energy because it contains many more water molecules.

When you put ice cubes in a pitcher of lemonade, energy is transferred from the warmer lemonade to the colder ice. The thermal energy of the lemonade decreases, and the thermal energy of the ice increases. Because the particles in the lemonade have transferred some of their thermal energy to the ice molecules, the average kinetic energy of the lemonade particles decreases. Therefore, the temperature of the lemonade decreases. **Heat** is the energy transferred from an object at a higher temperature to an object at a lower temperature.

When two objects at different temperatures come into contact, energy is always transferred from the object that has the higher temperature to the object that has the lower temperature. Energy in the form of heat always flows from hot to cold.

Another example of heat flow is putting food in a hot insulated cooler. We use insulated coolers to keep our food cold, but if cold food is placed in a hot insulated cooler that has been out in the sun, the food will get warmer.

This happens because the heat flows from the insulated cooler to the food, until the food and the insulated cooler are the same temperature. This is the opposite effect that is desired when using an insulated cooler. The solution to keep food cool is to put ice in the insulated cooler before placing the food inside. Once the ice is in the insulated cooler, the heat from the food will flow to the ice, cause it to melt, and in turn keep the food cool.

Adding or removing heat from a substance will affect its temperature and thermal energy. Heat, however, is not the same as thermal energy and temperature. These are properties of a substance. Heat is the energy involved when these properties change.

Energy and Changes in State

The matter that makes up a frozen juice bar is the same whether the juice bar is frozen or has melted. The matter is just in a different form, or state. Remember that the kinetic theory of matter states that the particles that make up matter move around at different speeds. The state of a substance depends on the speed of its particles. Adding energy in the form of heat to a substance may result in a change of state. The added energy may cause the bonds between particles to break. This is what allows the state to change. Adding energy in the form of heat to a chunk of glacier may cause the ice to melt into water. Removing energy in the form of heat from a substance may also result in a change of state.

Student-Response Activity

1 What is temperature and how is it measured?

_____

_____

_____

_____

_____

❷ Pedro is examining photos of various samples of water all at 30°C. Which sample has the greatest thermal energy? Explain your answer.

_____

_____

❸ What happens to the bonds between particles when heat is added?

_____

_____

_____

❹ What happens when heat is added to a block of ice?

_____

_____

_____

❺ What happens to the temperature and thermal energy of water when it is heated in a pot on the stove?

_____

_____

_____

Benchmark Assessment SC.7.P.11.1, SC.7.P.11.4

Fill in the letter of the best choice.

1 What happens when heat is removed from a liquid?

(A)   The particles evaporate.

(B)   The particles speed up.

(C)   The temperature decreases.

(D)   The temperature increases.

2 Which statement about the kinetic molecular theory is **true**?

(F)   Particles in a liquid move around at higher speeds than in gases and solids.

(G)   Particles move in liquids and gases, but particles in a solid do not move.

(H)   Particles move in solids more than in liquids and gases.

(I)   Particles move the least in solids and the most in gases.

3 Which statement about heat is **true**?

(A)   Heat and temperature are the same property of an object.

(B)   Heat and thermal energy are the same property of an object.

(C)   Heat is the energy transferred from an object of high temperature to one of low temperature.

(D)   Heat measures the average kinetic energy of an object.

4 Which transition best shows how particle movement changes when heat is removed from a system?

W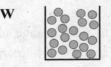

X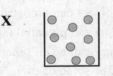

Y

Z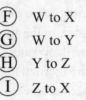

(F)   W to X

(G)   W to Y

(H)   Y to Z

(I)   Z to X

5 What happens to the particles in a cold, metal spoon when it is placed in a bowl of hot soup?

(A)   Particle movement does not change.

(B)   The particles move closer together.

(C)   The particles move faster.

(D)   The particles move slower.

SC.7.P.11.2 Investigate and describe the transformation of energy from one form to another.
SC.7.P.11.3 Cite evidence to explain that energy cannot be created nor destroyed, only changed from one form to another.

Energy Conversion and Conservation

Forms of Energy

Energy is the ability to cause change and do work. Energy is measured in joules (J). Energy can come in many different forms. Mechanical energy is the amount of work an object can do because of the object's kinetic (motion) and potential (stored) energies. Mechanical energy can be all potential energy, all kinetic energy, or some of each. The mechanical energy of an object remains the same unless it transfers some of its energy to another object. But even if the mechanical energy of an object stays the same, the potential energy or kinetic energy it has can increase or decrease.

Other forms of energy include thermal, chemical, electrical, sound, light, and nuclear energy. Thermal energy is all of the kinetic energy due to the random motion of the particles that make up an object. Thermal energy also depends on the number of particles. Water, in the form of steam, has a higher temperature than water in a lake does. But the lake has more thermal energy because the lake has more water particles.

Chemical energy is the energy of a compound that changes as its atoms are rearranged. Chemical energy is a form of potential energy because it depends on the position and arrangement of the atoms in a compound.

Electrical energy is the energy of moving electrons. The electrical energy used in your home comes from power plants. Huge generators turn magnets inside loops of wire. The changing position of a magnet makes electrical energy run

through the wire and along the wires from the power plants to electrical weigh stations to your home. This electrical energy is stored as potential energy until you use it to run your electrical appliances.

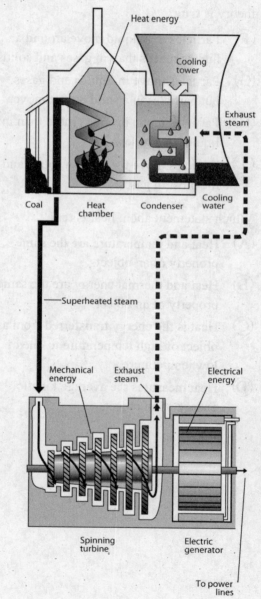

FSSA Review and Practice
© Houghton Mifflin Harcourt Publishing Company

Benchmark Review

Sound energy is caused by an object's vibrations. When you stretch a guitar string, the string stores potential energy. When you let the string go, this potential energy is turned into kinetic energy, which makes the string vibrate. The string also transmits some of this kinetic energy to the air around it. The air particles also vibrate and transmit this energy in the form of a wave to your ear. When the sound energy reaches your ear, you hear the sound of the guitar. Sound waves need a medium, such as air or wood, to travel through.

Electromagnetic energy is produced by the vibrations of electrically charged particles. It is transmitted in the form of an electromagnetic wave. Visible light is a type of electromagnetic energy. Other types include x-rays, ultraviolet light, and infrared light. The vibrations that transmit light energy do not need to be carried through matter. In fact, electromagnetic waves can move through a vacuum where there is no matter.

Energy Transformation

Energy transformation takes place when energy changes from one form into another form. Any form of energy can change into any other form of energy. Often, one form of energy changes into more than one form. For example, when you rub your hands together, you hear a sound, and your hands get warm. The kinetic energy of your moving hands transforms into both sound energy and thermal energy.

Another example of an energy transformation is when chemical energy is converted in the body. Why is eating breakfast so important? Eating breakfast gives your body the energy needed to help you start your day. Your chemical potential energy comes from the food you eat. Your body breaks down the components of the food to access the energy contained in them. This energy changes to the kinetic energy in your muscles. Some of the chemical energy converts to thermal energy that allows your body to stay warm.

Energy is Conserved in Transformations

A closed system is a group of objects that transfer energy only to one another. For example, a roller coaster can be considered a closed system if it includes everything involved, such as the track, the cars, and the air around them. Energy is conserved in all closed systems. The law of conservation of energy states that energy cannot be created or destroyed. It can only change form. All of the different forms of energy in a closed system always add up to the same total amount of energy. It does not matter how many energy conversions take place.

For example, on a roller coaster some mechanical energy gets transformed into sound and thermal energy as it goes down a hill. The total of the coaster's reduced mechanical energy at the bottom of the hill, the increased thermal energy, and the sound energy is the same amount of energy as the original amount of mechanical energy. In other words, total energy is conserved.

Student-Response Activity

❶ What is mechanical energy?

_____

_____

❷ Television remote controls use infrared light to send a signal. What type of energy is infrared light?

_____

_____

❸ Describe the energy transfer that happens when you plug in a blender.

_____

_____

❹ Explain why you hear a sound when you rub your hands together.

_____

_____

_____

❺ Complete the Venn diagram to compare and contrast sound energy and electromagnetic energy.

Sound Energy   Both   Electromagnetic Energy

Benchmark Assessment SC.7.P.11.2, SC.7.P.11.3

Fill in the letter of the best choice.

 1 Which item converts electrical energy into thermal energy?

- (A) burning log
- (B) microwave
- (C) plant
- (D) radio

2 Which type of energy do the compounds in the food we eat contain?

- (F) chemical energy
- (G) electromagnetic energy
- (H) kinetic energy
- (I) thermal energy

 3 Which type of energy causes your eardrum to vibrate?

- (A) chemical
- (B) electrical
- (C) sound
- (D) thermal

4 Which statement is **true** about energy in a flashlight?

- (F) Chemical energy is converted to electrical energy.
- (G) Energy is not conserved during energy transformations.
- (H) Energy is not transformed in a flashlight.
- (I) Light energy that is produced cannot travel in the air.

5 Which statement about the law of conservation of energy is **true**?

- (A) Chemical energy is conserved, but light energy is destroyed.
- (B) Energy is always conserved as long as the system is closed.
- (C) Energy is only conserved for two transformations within a system.
- (D) Potential energy is conserved, but kinetic energy is destroyed.

> **SC.6.P.12.1** Measure and graph distance versus time for an object moving at a constant speed. Interpret this relationship. **SC.6.P.13.3** Investigate and describe that an unbalanced force acting on an object changes its speed, or direction of motion, or both.

Unbalanced Forces, Motion, and Speed

Describing Location

Have you ever gotten lost while looking for a specific place? If so, you probably know that the description of the location can be very important. Suppose you are trying to describe your location to a friend. How would you explain where you are? You need two pieces of information: a position and a reference point.

With a Position

Position describes the location of an object. Often, you describe where something is by comparing its position with where you currently are. For example, you might say that a classmate sitting next to you is two desks to your right, or that a mailbox is two blocks south of where you live. Each time you identify the position of an object, you are comparing the location of the object with the location of another object or place.

With a Reference Point

When you describe a position by comparing it to the location of another object or place, you are using a reference point. A **reference point** is a location to which you compare other locations. In the mailbox example above, the reference point is "where you live." Suppose you are at a zoo with some friends. If you are using the map to the right, you could describe your destination using different reference points. Using yourself as the reference point, you might say that the red panda house is one block east and three blocks north of your current location. Or you might say the red panda

house is one block north and one block east of the fountain. In this example, the fountain is your reference point.

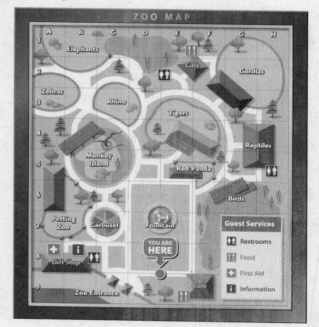

What Is Motion?

An object moves, or is in motion, when it changes its position relative to a reference point. **Motion** is a change in position over time. If you were to watch a girl on a bike, you would see her move. If you were not able to watch her, you might still know something about her motion. If you saw that the biker was in one place at one time and a different place later, you would know that she had moved. A change in position is evidence that motion has happened. If the biker returned to her starting point, you might not know that she had moved. The starting and ending positions cannot tell you everything about motion.

What Is Speed?

A change in an object's position tells you that motion took place, but it does not tell you how quickly the object changed position. The **speed** of an object is a measure of how far something moves in a given amount of time. In other words, speed measures how quickly or slowly the object changes position. In the same amount of time, a faster object would move farther than a slower moving object. The speed of an object is rarely constant. For example, a biker may travel quickly when she begins a race, but may slow down as she gets tired at the end of the race. Average speed is a way to calculate the speed of an object that may not always be moving at a constant speed. Instead of describing the speed of an object at an exact moment, average speed describes the speed over a stretch of time.

Graphing Constant Speed

A convenient way to show the motion of an object is by using a graph that plots the distance the object has traveled against time. This type of graph is called a distance-time graph. You can use it to see how both distance and speed change with time.

How far away the object is from a reference point is plotted on the y-axis. So the y-axis expresses distance in units such as meters, centimeters, or kilometers. Time is plotted on the x-axis, and can display units such as seconds, minutes, or hours. If an object moves at a constant speed, the graph is a straight line.

You can use a distance-time graph to determine the average speed of an object. The slope, or steepness, of the line is equal to the average speed of the object. You calculate the average speed for a time interval by dividing the change in distance by the change in time for that time interval.

Suppose that a horse is running at a constant speed. The distance-time graph of its motion is shown below. To calculate the speed of the horse, choose two data points from the graph below and calculate the slope of the line. The calculation of the slope uses the change in y (140 m -70 m) divided by the change in x (10 s - 5 s). Since we know that the slope of a line on a distance-time graph is its average speed, then we know that the horse's speed is 14 m/s.

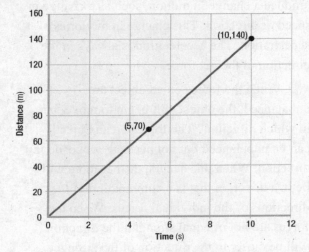

How are changing speeds graphed? Some distance-time graphs show the motion of an object with a changing speed. In these distance-time graphs, the change in the slope of a line indicates that the object has sped up, slowed down, or stopped.

As an object moves, the distance it travels increases with time. The motion can be seen as a climbing line on the graph. The slope of the line indicates speed. Steeper lines show intervals where the speed is greater than intervals with less steep lines. If the line gets steeper, the object is speeding up. If the line gets less steep, the object is slowing. If the line becomes flat, or horizontal, the object is not moving. In this interval, the speed is zero meters per second.

Changes in Speed or Direction

When the forces on an object produce a net force of 0 N, the forces are balanced. **Balanced forces** will not cause a change in the motion of a moving object, and they will not cause a nonmoving object to start moving. Many objects around you have only balanced forces acting on them. When the net force is not 0 N, the forces on the object are unbalanced. **Unbalanced forces** produce a change in motion, such as a change in speed or direction. This change in motion is acceleration. The acceleration is always in the direction of the net force.

When the forces on an object are unbalanced, the object will begin to move, but in which direction? The forces on an object can be unbalanced but not perfectly opposite in direction. When this occurs, the net force will be in a direction that is a combination of the directions of the individual forces. When the forces are not of equal strength, the direction will be closer to the direction of the stronger force.

Forces Act on Objects

You know that force and motion are related. When you exert a force on a football by kicking it with your foot, or throwing it in the air, the ball will change its motion. In the 1680s, Sir Isaac Newton explained this relationship between force and motion with three laws of motion. Newton's first law describes the motion of an object that has a net force of 0 N acting on it. The law states: *An object at rest remains at rest, and an object in motion maintains its velocity unless it experiences an unbalanced force.* This law is easier to understand when broken down into parts.

An object at rest remains at rest . . . unless it experiences an unbalanced force. An object that is not moving is said to be at rest. A desk in a classroom, or a football on a kicking tee, are both examples of objects at rest. Newton's

first law says that objects at rest will stay at rest unless acted on by an unbalanced force. An object will not start moving until a push or a pull is exerted upon it. So, a desk will not slide across the floor unless a force pushes the desk, and a football will not move off the tee until a force pushes, or kicks, it off. Nothing at rest starts moving until a force makes it move.

An object in motion maintains its velocity unless it experiences an unbalanced force. The second part of Newton's first law is about objects with a certain velocity. Such objects will continue to move forever with the same velocity unless an unbalanced force acts on them. Think about coming to a sudden stop while riding a bike. The bike comes to a stop when the brakes are applied. But your body feels like it is moving forward, so you must hold and push back against the handlebars forcing the motion of your body to stop with the bike. These two parts of the law are really stating the same thing. Remember that an object at rest has a velocity—its velocity is zero.

Newton's first law is also called the law of inertia. **Inertia** is the tendency of all objects to resist any change in motion. Because of inertia, an object at rest will remain at rest until a force makes it move. Likewise, inertia is why a moving object will maintain its velocity until a force changes its speed or direction. Inertia is why it is impossible for a bicycle, a car, or a train to stop immediately.

Acceleration

When an unbalanced force acts on an object, the object moves with accelerated motion. Newton's second law describes the motion: *The acceleration of an object depends on the mass of the object and the amount of force applied.* This law links force, mass, and acceleration. Suppose you are pushing a wagon. When the wagon is empty, it has less mass, so your force accelerates the wagon quickly. But when someone is sitting in the wagon, the same push accelerates the wagon more slowly.

Student-Response Activity

1 What are two pieces of information that are needed to describe the location of an object?

_____

_____

2 When two forces acting on a moving object are unbalanced, what can happen to this object?

_____

_____

3 Joe and Toby both rode their bikes to the library. They left their homes at noon and both arrived at the same time. Examine the map below that shows the location of Joe's house, Toby's house, and the library. Who traveled at the greater speed? Explain your answer.

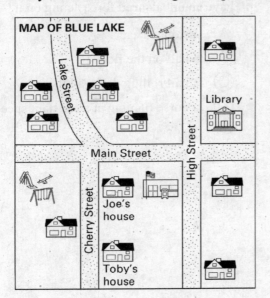

_____

_____

_____

_____

_____

_____

_____

4 Explain the movement of the zebra in your own words.

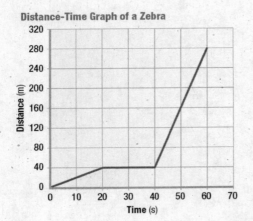

_____

_____

_____

_____

_____

Benchmark Assessment SC.6.P.12.1, SC.6.P.13.3

Fill in the letter of the best choice.

A student examines a distance-time graph of a squirrel. Use this graph to answer Questions 1–3.

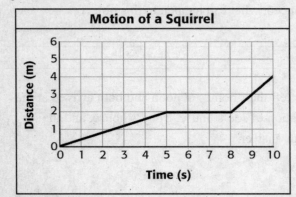

Motion of a Squirrel

❶ During which time interval is the squirrel traveling at the fastest speed?

Ⓐ 1–2 min

Ⓑ 2–3 min

Ⓒ 5–6 min

Ⓓ 8–9 min

❷ At which point does the squirrel stop moving?

Ⓕ 1–2 min

Ⓖ 2–3 min

Ⓗ 5–8 min

Ⓘ 9–10 min

❸ During which time interval did the squirrel travel the farthest?

Ⓐ 1–2 min

Ⓑ 3–4 min

Ⓒ 5–8 min

Ⓓ 8–10 min

❹ The motion of four cars is described below. Which car has the highest speed?

Ⓕ a car that travels 10 km in 0.5 hour

Ⓖ a car that travels 15 km in 1 hour

Ⓗ a car that travels 20 km in 1 hour

Ⓘ a car that travels 30 km in 0.5 hour

❺ Unbalanced forces cause a change in speed, motion, or both. Which must have an unbalanced force acting on it?

Ⓐ a stopped car

Ⓑ a ball on the floor

Ⓒ a ball rolling down a hill

Ⓓ a horse running at a constant speed

> **SC.6.P.13.1** Investigate and describe types of forces, including contact forces and forces acting at a distance, such as electrical, magnetic, and gravitational. **SC.6.P.13.2** Explore the Law of Gravity by recognizing that every object exerts gravitational force on every other object and that the force depends on how much mass the objects have and how far apart they are.

Types of Forces

Force

In science, a **force** is simply a push or a pull. Forces are vectors, meaning that they have both a magnitude and a direction. A force can cause an object to accelerate, and thereby change the speed or direction of motion. In fact, when you see a change in an object's motion, you can infer that one or more forces acted on the object. These forces are said to be unbalanced because they are unequal in size. When an object is not changing speed or direction in motion it means that there are balanced forces acting on it. These forces are equal in size but opposite in direction.

The unit that measures force is the newton (N). One newton is equal to one kilogram-meter per second squared (kg•m/s^2).

All forces exist only when there is something for them to act on. However, a force can act on an object without causing a change in motion. For example, when you sit on a chair, the downward force you exert on the chair does not cause the chair to move, because the floor exerts a counteracting upward force on the chair.

How Do Forces Act?

It is not always easy to tell what is exerting a force or what is acted on by a force. Forces can be contact forces, as when one object touches or bumps into another. When you use your muscles to push on a box to move it, you exert a contact force on the box.

Another type of contact force is friction. Friction happens when one object that is moving touches another object. Friction causes some of the energy of motion to become heat energy. This energy transformation causes the object to slow down. Air resistance is a type of friction that happens when an object moves through the air.

Forces can also act at a distance. Magnetic force is an example of a force that can act at a distance. The magnet does not have to be directly touching the metal to be held to it. A magnetic force can hold a magnet to a refrigerator even when there is something in the way, such as paper or a photograph.

Electrical forces are another type of force that acts over a distance. Particles of opposite charge are pulled towards each other. Particles of the same charge are pushed away from each other. If you have ever gotten a shock when you touch a doorknob after shuffling along the carpet, you have felt an electrical force. As you move along the carpet, your shoes pick up loose electrons. Electrons have a negative charge. When you touch the metal doorknob, the electrons jump off you and onto the metal.

The Force of Gravity

When you jump up, a force called gravity pulls you back to the ground even though you are separated from Earth.

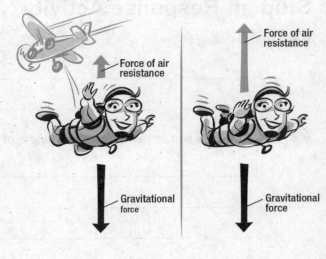

Force of air resistance

Gravitational force

Force of air resistance

Gravitational force

If you watch a video of astronauts on the moon, you will see them wearing big, bulky spacesuits, yet jumping lightly. Why is leaping on the moon easier than on Earth? The answer is gravity. Gravity is a force of attraction between objects due to their mass. Gravity is a noncontact force that acts between two objects at any distance apart.

The law of universal gravitation relates gravitational force, mass, and distance. It states that all objects attract each other through gravitational force. The strength of the force depends on the masses involved and distance between them.

The gravitational force between two objects increases as the distance between their centers decreases. This means that objects far apart have a weaker attraction than objects close together. If two objects move closer, the attraction between them increases. For example, you cannot feel the sun's gravity because it is so far away, but if you were able to stand on the surface of the sun, you would find it impossible to move due to the gravity!

The gravitational force between two objects increases with the mass of each object. This means that objects with greater mass have more attraction between them. A cow has more mass than a cat, so there is more attraction between the Earth and the cow, and the cow weighs more. This part of the law of universal gravitation explains why astronauts on the moon bounce when they walk. The moon has less mass than Earth, so the astronauts weigh less. The force of each step pushes an astronaut higher than it would on Earth.

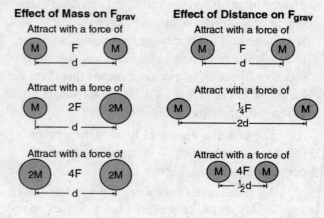

Student-Response Activity

❶ What is a force?

_____

_____

❷ What are two factors that affect the strength of gravitational force between two objects?

_____

_____

_____

_____

❸ Complete the Venn diagram to compare contact forces and forces that act over a distance.

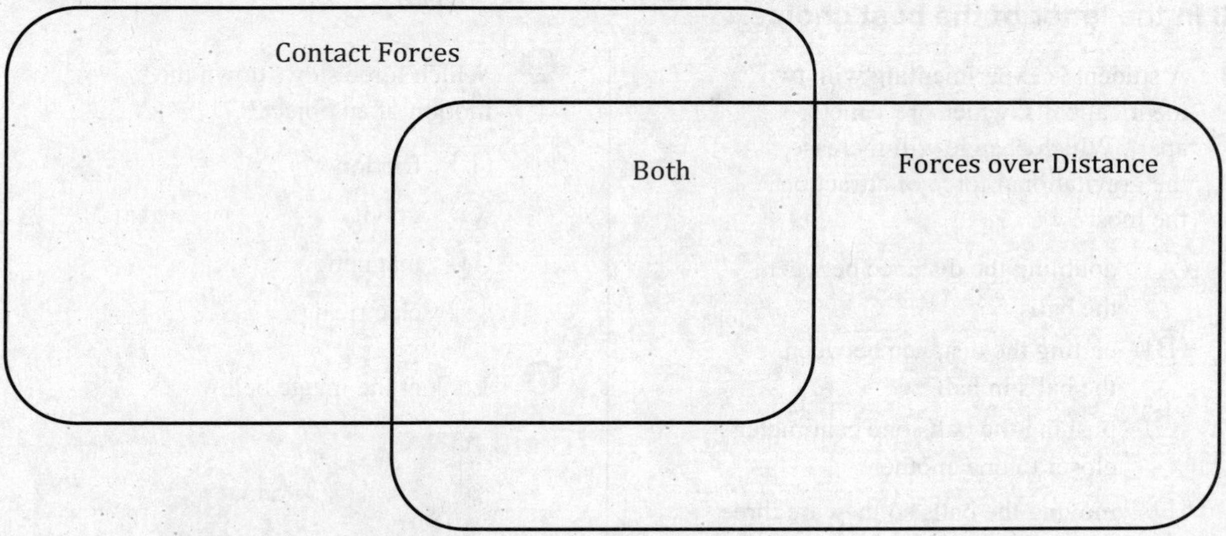

Contact Forces

Both

Forces over Distance

❹ Suzanna notices that when she rolls a marble on the carpet, the marble slows down and stops. What force causes the marble to change its motion? How does this force act?

_____

_____

_____

_____

_____

_____

❺ Explain the difference between balanced and unbalanced forces.

_____

_____

_____

_____

_____

Benchmark Assessment SC.6.P.13.1, SC.6.P.13.2

Fill in the letter of the best choice.

1 A student is experimenting with two identical balls, which are 1 meter apart. Which change will increase the gravitational force of attraction the most?

(A) doubling the distance between the balls

(B) cutting the distance between the balls in half

(C) pushing the balls one centimeter closer to one another

(D) moving the balls so they are three meters apart from one another

2 Ignacio uses a hammer to hit a nail into a board on the floor. How does gravity make it easier to hammer the nail?

(F) Gravity pushes the board up to help the nail go in.

(G) Gravity pulls the board and the nail toward one another.

(H) Gravity pulls the hammer down so it pushes on the nail.

(I) Gravity pulls the nail down, but it does not pull on the hammer.

3 Which force attracts all matter together?

(A) friction

(B) gravity

(C) magnetic

(D) electrical

4 Which force slows down the motion of an object?

(F) friction

(G) gravity

(H) magnetic

(I) electrical

5 Look at the image below.

Which force holds the paper to the refrigerator?

(A) friction

(B) gravity

(C) magnetic

(D) electrical

> **SC.6.L.14.1** Describe and identify patterns in the hierarchical organization of organisms from atoms to molecules and cells to tissues to organs to organ systems to organisms.

Cellular Organization

The Smallest Particles

All matter in the universe, including living matter, is made from tiny particles called **atoms**. Atoms are made up of exactly one type of matter, such as hydrogen or oxygen. **Molecules** are the smallest unit of matter of a substance that retains all the physical and chemical properties of that substance. Molecules can consist of a single atom or a group of atoms bonded together. Water molecules, for example, are made up of two hydrogen atoms and one oxygen atom. Atoms and molecules are essential to all living things.

Cells

An **organism** is a living thing that can carry out life processes by itself. Unicellular organisms are made up of just one cell that performs all of the functions necessary for life. Having only one cell has advantages and disadvantages. For example, unicellular organisms need fewer resources. Some can live in harsh conditions, such as hot springs and very salty water. However, unicellular organisms are very small, which means they may be eaten by larger organisms. Another disadvantage of being unicellular is that the entire organism dies if the single cell dies.

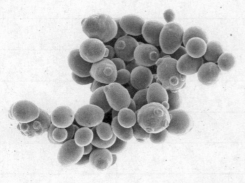

Multicellular organisms are made up of more than one cell. These cells are grouped into different levels of organization, including tissues, organs, and organ systems. The cells that make up a multicellular organism, such as humans and plants, may be specialized to perform specific functions. Different cells have different functions in the body. This specialization makes the multicellular organism more efficient. Other benefits of being multicellular are larger size and longer life span. There are disadvantages to being multicellular, too. Multicellular organisms need more resources than unicellular organisms do. Also, the cells of multicellular organisms are specialized for certain jobs, which means that cells must depend on each other to perform all of the functions that an organism needs. A multicellular organism can have four levels of organization: cells, tissues, organs, and organ systems.

Tissues

A tissue is a group of similar cells that perform a common function. Most animals are made of four basic types of tissues: nervous, epithelial, connective, and muscle. The function of nervous tissue is to pass messages around the body. Epithelial tissue protects the body by forming boundaries, such as linings of organs. Connective tissue is responsible for holding parts of the body together and for supporting and nourishing organs. Muscle tissue is responsible for movement.

Plants are made of different types of tissues than animals. The three types of tissues that plants contain are transport, protective, and ground. Water and nutrients are moved through the plant by protective tissues. Protective tissues protect the outside of the plant. Ground tissues are responsible for supporting the plant and storage.

Organs

An **organ** is a structure made up of a collection of tissues that carries out a specialized function. The heart is an organ that pumps blood containing nutrients and oxygen around the body. Multiple types of tissues must work together for organs to function. For example, nervous tissue sends messages to muscle tissue in the heart to tell the muscle tissue to contract. When the muscle tissue contracts, the heart pumps blood throughout the body.

Plants also contain organs that require different tissue types to work together. A leaf is an organ that contains all three types of plant tissues. The leaf is able to reduce water loss because of its protective tissue. The ground tissue in the leaf is used for photosynthesis. Nutrients are distributed from the leaves to the stems by transport tissue.

Organ Systems

An **organ system** is a group of organs that work together to perform body functions. Each organ system has a specific job to do for the organism. For example, the stomach works with other organs of the digestive system to digest and absorb nutrients from food. Other organs included in the digestive system are the esophagus and the small and large intestines. The diagram below shows the organs of the digestive system.

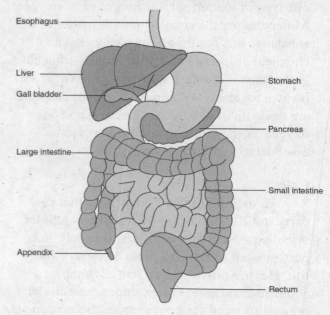

Esophagus
Liver
Gall bladder
Large intestine
Appendix
Stomach
Pancreas
Small intestine
Rectum

Student-Response Activity

❶ What are the levels of organization in multicellular organisms?

_____

_____

_____

_____

_____

❷ Fill in the Venn diagram to compare the functions of animal tissues and plant tissues. What functions do they share?

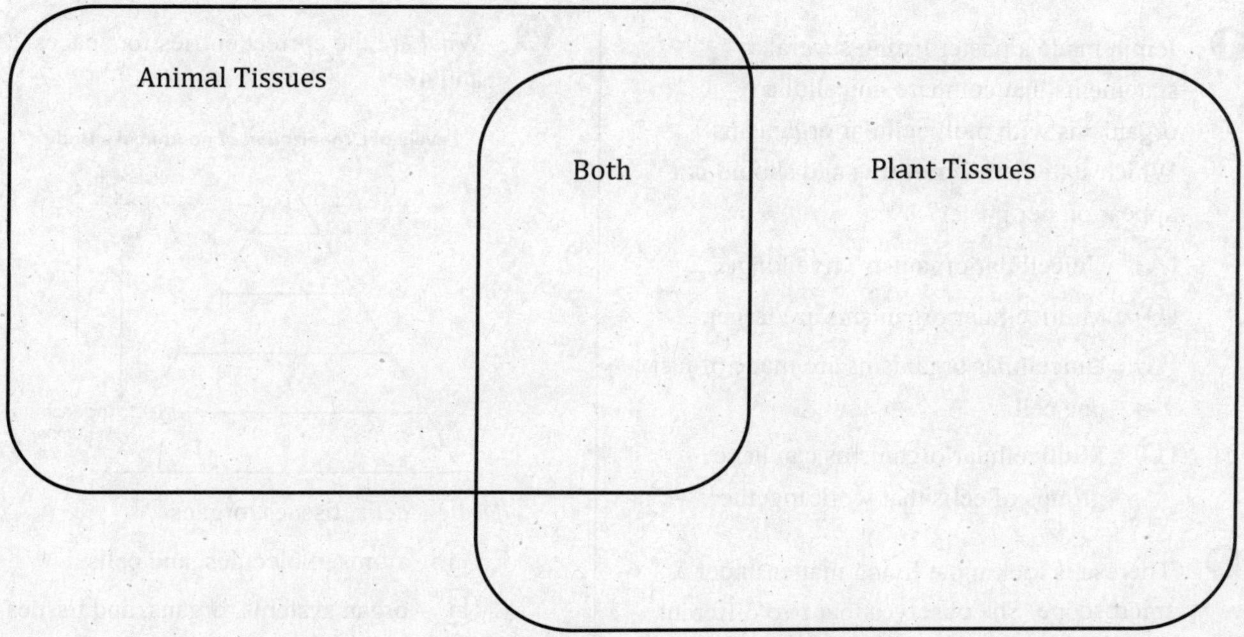

Animal Tissues

Both

Plant Tissues

❸ What are two benefits of multicellular organisms having some specialized cells rather than all the cells being the same?

_____

_____

_____

_____

❹ How can you compare a bicycle to an organism? Identify parts of a bicycle that are comparable to tissues, organs, and organ systems.

_____

_____

_____

_____

_____

Benchmark Assessment SC.6.L.14.1

Fill in the letter of the best choice.

❶ Jemin made a poster listing several statements that compare unicellular organisms with multicellular organisms. Which statement is **not** true and should not appear on her poster?

(A) Unicellular organisms live longer.

(B) Multicellular organisms are larger.

(C) Unicellular organisms are made of just one cell.

(D) Multicellular organisms can have groups of cells that work together.

❷ Theresa is looking at living matter under a microscope. She observes that two different types of cells are present in one structure. What is the **most** complex level of organization that Theresa is observing?

(F) cell

(G) molecule

(H) organ

(I) tissue

❸ Xavier observes a group of similar cells that are working together to produce a substance. What kind of structure is he observing?

(A) molecule

(B) organ

(C) organ system

(D) tissue

❹ What are the correct entries for spaces 2, 3, and 4?

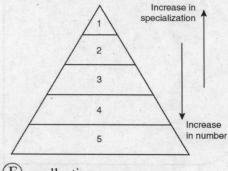

Levels of Organization of an Animal's Body

(F) cells, tissues, organs

(G) atoms, molecules, and cells

(H) organ systems, organs, and tissues

(I) organs, organ systems, and organisms

❺ Green algae in the genus *Volvox* is formed by cells that join together. Each cell can survive on its own, but the cells work together to survive better. Which statement **correctly** explains how *Volvox* should be classified?

(A) They are unicellular organisms because each cell can survive on its own.

(B) They are unicellular organisms because each cell contains its own DNA.

(C) They are unicellular organisms because each cell performs a different function.

(D) They are unicellular organisms because each cell is part of a collection of cells.

SC.6.L.14.2 Investigate and explain the components of the scientific theory of cells (cell theory): all organisms are composed of cells (single-celled or multi-cellular), all cells come from pre-existing cells, and cells are the basic unit of life. **SC.6.L.14.3** Recognize and explore how cells of all organisms undergo similar processes to maintain homeostasis, including extracting energy from food, getting rid of waste, and reproducing.

Characteristics of Cells

Cells Are Everywhere

Like all living things, you are made up of cells. A **cell** is the smallest functional and structural unit of all living organisms, and all organisms are made up of cells. Some organisms are just one cell. Others, such as humans, contain trillions of cells. An organism carries out all of its own life processes.

Organisms that are made up of just one cell are called *unicellular organisms*. The single cell of a unicellular organism must carry out all of the functions for life. Organisms that are made up of more than one cell are called *multicellular organisms*. The cells of multicellular organisms often have specialized structures and functions.

How Cells Were Discovered

In the early 1600s, nobody knew what a cell was. In 1665, a scientist named Robert Hooke built a microscope to look at tiny objects. One day, he looked at a thin slice of cork from the bark of a cork tree. The cork looked as if it was made of little boxes. Hooke named these boxes *cells*, which means "little rooms" in Latin. Around 1674, Anton van Leeuwenhoek became the first person to describe actual living cells when he looked at a drop of pond water under a microscope. He observed tiny organisms moving through the water. These early discoveries laid the foundations for what is known today as cell theory.

Plant Cells

In 1838, Matthias Schleiden concluded that plants are made of cells. Then in 1839, Theodor Schwann determined that all animal tissues are made of cells. He concluded that all organisms are made up of one or more cells. Based on his observations about the cellular make up of organisms, Schwann made another conclusion. He determined that the cell is the basic unit of all living things. In 1858, Rudolf Virchow, a doctor, proposed that cells could form only from the division of other cells. The work of Schleiden, Schwann, and Virchow resulted in a scientific theory of cells.

The cell theory is fundamental to the study of organisms, medicine, heredity, evolution, and all other aspects of life science. Based on the evidence collected by scientists, the cell theory lists three basic characteristics of all cells and organisms:

- All organisms are made up of one or more cells.
- The cell is the basic unit of all organisms.
- All cells come from existing cells.

What Cells Have in Common

Scientific research has shown that cells are the basic unit of life. This means that cells carry out all of the functions necessary to keep an organism living. In order for cells to survive, they need to obtain and use energy, eliminate wastes, exchange materials, and make new cells. These processes allow cells to maintain the right balance of materials and conditions inside of themselves. The maintenance of a constant internal state in a changing environment is called **homeostasis**. Homeostasis allows cells and organisms to stay alive.

All living things need food to produce energy for cell processes. The process by which cells use oxygen to produce energy from food is called cellular respiration. Plants, animals, and most other organisms use cellular respiration to get energy from food.

Nearly all the oxygen around us is made by photosynthesis. Animals and plants use oxygen during cellular respiration to break down food. Cellular respiration also produces carbon dioxide. Plants need carbon dioxide to make sugars. So, photosynthesis and respiration are linked, each one depending on the products of the other.

Different cells vary in size and shape. However, all cells have some parts in common, including cell membranes, cytoplasm, organelles, and DNA. These different parts help the cell to carry out all the tasks needed for life.

How Cells Can Differ

Although cells have some basic parts in common, there are some important differences. The way that cells store their DNA is the main difference between the two cell types.

A **eukaryote** is an organism made up of cells that contain their DNA in a nucleus. All multicellular organisms are eukaryotes. Most eukaryotes are multicellular. Some eukaryotes, such as amoebas and yeasts, are unicellular. Eukaryotic cells contain membrane-bound organelles, as well as ribosomes.

eukaryotic cell

Not all eukaryotic cells are the same. Animals, plants, protists, and fungi are eukaryotes. Cells from these different types of organisms can be identified by some of their structures. For example, plants have a cell wall outside of their cell membrane, but

animal cells do not. Fungi cells have cell walls that are different from plant cell walls. Protist cells may or may not have cell walls. Plant cells are also distinguished by having chloroplasts, which allows them to perform photosynthesis.

prokaryotic cell

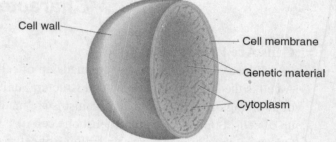

Cell wall — Cell membrane — Genetic material — Cytoplasm

A **prokaryote** is a single-celled organism that does not have a nucleus or membrane-bound organelles. Its DNA is located in the cytoplasm. Prokaryotic cells contain organelles called ribosomes that do not have a membrane. Some prokaryotic cells have hair-like structures called *flagella* that help them move. Prokaryotes, which include all bacteria and archaea, are almost always smaller than eukaryotes.

Cells Maintain Homeostasis

In order for cells to stay alive, they must maintain **homeostasis**, which is the maintenance of a constant internal state in a changing environment. They do this in similar ways. All cells require energy to perform their cell functions. Cells get energy from breaking down materials, such as food in which energy is stored. Plant cells make their own food through photosynthesis. They take in sunlight and change carbon dioxide and water into sugar and oxygen. Other organisms eat plants or other organisms that eat plants. Regardless of whether the organism makes its own food through photosynthesis or consumes another organism, they must all use oxygen to produce energy from their food. This is called **cellular respiration**.

It is also important that cells can get rid of wastes. This happens through the cell's membrane, which is semi-permeable. Only certain particles are allowed to cross the cell membrane. There are two types of transport through the cell membrane—

passive transport and active transport. **Passive transport** is the movement of particles across a cell membrane without the use of energy by the cell. One type of passive transport is called diffusion. This is when molecules move from high concentrations to low concentrations. Some waste products move out of the cell by diffusion. When cells need to move materials across the cell membrane from areas of low concentration to areas of higher concentration, they use active transport. **Active transport** is the movement of particles against a concentration gradient and requires the cell to use energy. Sometimes large particles require active transport to move them across a cell membrane.

Maintaining homeostasis also means that cells grow, divide and die. Multicellular organisms grow by adding more cells, which are made when existing cells divide. Some cells divide often to replace dead or damaged cells. Cell division is required for growth. Before the cell can divide, the DNA needs to be copied and separated. The DNA is packaged into chromosomes before they can divide. When equal numbers of chromosomes are separated, and the nucleus splits to form two identical nuclei, this is called **mitosis**. After mitosis occurs, the rest of the cell divides. Now there are two identical cells.

Student-Response Activity

1 Read each evidence statement. Which part of cell theory is supported by each piece of evidence?

Cells can be observed in plants, animals, fungi, protists, bacteria, and archaea.

_____
_____

A scientist observes two petri dishes. A colony of bacteria grows in one, and nothing grows in the other.

_____
_____

A single cell from a multicellular plant can be kept alive.

_____
_____

2 A scientist discovers a type of cell that produces a chemical, which is not useful to the cell. What can you conclude about the cell?

_____
_____
_____
_____

3 What are four things that cells can do to maintain homeostasis?

_____

_____

_____

_____

4 Use the terms listed in the word bank to fill in the blanks with the matching cell parts in each cell. Some terms may be used more than once.

Word Bank	Eukaryotes	Prokaryotes
cytoplasm	_____	_____
cell membrane	_____	_____
DNA in cytoplasm	_____	_____
DNA in nucleus	_____	_____
membrane-bound organelles	_____	_____
organelles	_____	_____

5 Paul and Jessica are making a model of an animal cell. What should they show going into and out of the cell in their model?

_____

_____

_____

_____

_____

Benchmark Assessment SC.6.L.14.2, SC.6.L.14.3

Fill in the letter of the best choice.

1 Eukaryotic cells and prokaryotic cells have some parts in common. Which pairs of parts would you find in **both** types of cells?

(A) cytoplasm and nucleus

(B) cell membrane and cytoplasm

(C) DNA and membrane-bound organelles

(D) cell membrane and membrane-bound organelles

2 A virus is made of a protein shell that carries DNA. Which statement **best** describes how the virus can be classified according to cell theory?

(F) It is an organism because it carries DNA.

(G) It is an organism because it can replicate itself.

(H) It is not an organism because it is not found in all living things.

(I) It is not an organism because it does not carry out all the functions of life.

3 Anthony places a drop of water under a microscope and observes some small objects. He concludes that the small objects are cells. Which choice **most likely** describes the evidence that Anthony saw?

(A) Anthony observed the objects moving in the water.

(B) Anthony observed the objects changing size and shape.

(C) Anthony observed the objects splitting into new objects.

(D) Anthony observed the objects sticking to one another.

4 Scientists observe that colonies of cells appear after a single cell is placed on a petri dish. Which statement does this evidence **best** support?

(F) Cells are able to reproduce.

(G) Cells are the basic unit of life.

(H) Cells are able to take in energy.

(I) Cells are able to get rid of waste.

5 Cells in a multicellular organism are shown in the diagram.

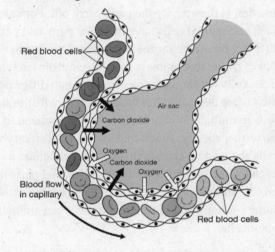

Which statement **best** describes how all of the cells shown are similar?

(A) They are all making new cells.

(B) They are all transporting oxygen.

(C) They are all doing photosynthesis.

(D) They are all maintaining homeostasis.

SC.6.L.14.4 Compare and contrast the structure and function of major organelles of plant and animal cells, including cell wall, cell membrane, nucleus, cytoplasm, chloroplasts, mitochondria, and vacuoles.

Cell Structure and Function

A Variety of Cells

All organisms are made up of one or more cells. Prokaryotes are made up of a single prokaryotic cell while eukaryotes are made up of one or more eukaryotic cells. Prokaryotic cells differ from eukaryotic cells in that they don't have a nucleus or membrane-bound organelles.

Eukaryotic cells can differ from each other depending on their structure and function. A cell's structure is the arrangement of its parts. A cell's function is the activity the parts carry out. For example, plant and animal cells have different parts that perform different functions for the organism. This is what makes plants and animals so different from each other. Even cells within the same organism can differ from each other depending on their function. Most of the cells in multicellular organisms are specialized to perform a specific function. However, all eukaryotic cells share some characteristics. These include a nucleus, membrane-bound organelles, and parts that protect and support the cell. The diagram below shows some similarities and differences between animal and plant cells.

Animal Cell and Plant Cell

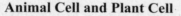
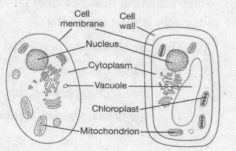

Cell Membrane

Every cell is surrounded by a cell membrane. The **cell membrane** acts as a barrier between the inside of a cell and the cell's environment. The cell membrane protects the cell and regulates what enters and leaves the cell.

Cell Wall

In addition to the cell membrane, plant cells have a cell wall. The **cell wall** is a rigid structure that surrounds the cell membrane. Cell walls provide support and protection to the cell. Plants don't have a skeleton like many animals do, so they get their shape from the cell wall. The cells of fungi, archaea, bacteria, and some protists also have cell walls.

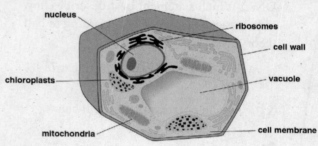

Nucleus

The nucleus is an organelle in eukaryotic cells that contains the cell's genetic material. Deoxyribonucleic acid, or DNA, is stored in the nucleus. DNA is genetic material that contains information needed for cell processes, such as making proteins. Proteins perform most actions of a cell. Although DNA is found in the nucleus, proteins are not made there. Instead, instructions for how to make proteins are stored in DNA. These instructions are sent out of the nucleus through pores in the nuclear membrane. The nuclear membrane is a double layer. Each layer is similar in structure to the cell membrane.

Cytoplasm

The **cytoplasm** is the region between the cell membrane and the nucleus that includes fluid and all of the organelles. Throughout the cytoplasm of eukaryotic cells is a cytoskeleton. The cytoskeleton is a network of protein filaments that gives shape and support to cells. The cytoskeleton is also involved in cell division and in movement. It may help parts within the cell to move. Or it may form structures that help the whole organism to move.

Chloroplasts

Animals must eat food to provide their cells with energy. However, plants, and some protists, can make their own food using photosynthesis. These organisms have **chloroplasts**, organelles where photosynthesis occurs. Photosynthesis is the process by which cells use sunlight, carbon dioxide, and water to make sugar and oxygen. Chloroplasts are green because they contain a green pigment called chlorophyll. Chlorophyll absorbs the energy in sunlight. This energy is used to make sugar, which is then used by mitochondria to make a molecule called adenosine triphosphate, or ATP. Similar to mitochondria, chloroplasts have two membranes and their own DNA.

Mitochondria

Organisms need energy for life processes. Cells carry out such processes for growth and repair, movement of materials into and out of the cell, and chemical processes. Cells get energy by breaking down food using a process called cellular respiration. Cellular respiration occurs in an organelle called the mitochondrion. In cellular respiration, cells use oxygen to release energy stored in food. For example, cells break down the sugar glucose to release the energy stored in the sugar. The mitochondria then transfer the energy released from the sugar to ATP. Cells use ATP to carry out cell processes.

Mitochondria have their own DNA and they have two membranes. The outer membrane is smooth. The inner membrane has many folds. Folds increase the surface area inside the mitochondria where cellular respiration occurs.

Vacuoles

A **vacuole** is a fluid-filled vesicle found in the cells of most animals, plants, and fungi. A vacuole may contain enzymes, nutrients, water, or wastes. Plant cells also have a large central vacuole that stores water. Central vacuoles full of water help support the cell. Plants may wilt when the central vacuole loses water.

Animal cells also have other structures similar to vacuoles called lysosomes. Lysosomes contain digestive enzymes, which break down worn-out or damaged organelles, waste materials, and foreign invaders in the cell. Some of these materials are collected in vacuoles. A lysosome attaches to the vacuole and releases the digestive enzymes inside. Some of these materials are recycled and reused in the cell. For example, a human liver cell recycles half of its materials each week.

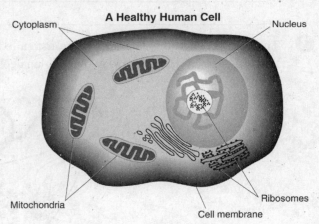

A Healthy Human Cell

Cytoplasm — Nucleus — Mitochondria — Cell membrane — Ribosomes

Student-Response Activity

1 Identify whether these statements describe an *animal cell*, a *plant cell*, or *both*.

nucleus: contains genetic material _____

lysosomes: helps to break down particles _____

chloroplasts: performs photosynthesis _____

mitochondria: releases energy through cellular respiration _____

cell wall: provides shape and support_____

cell membrane: separates the cell from its surroundings _____

central vacuole: stores water and helps support the cell_____

2 What are two adaptations in plant cells that do similar things for plants as bones do for animals?

_____

_____

3 The cell shown in the diagram is a protist called euglena. Early scientists were not sure how to classify this organism. What is one way that euglena cells are similar to plant cells, and one way they are similar to animal cells?

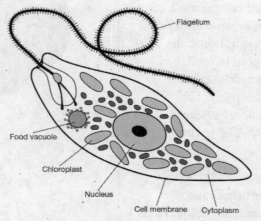

_____

_____

4 How are lysosomes similar to vacuoles?

_____

_____

5 A deer eats a leaf from a tree and gets energy from sugar molecules in the leaf. Which two organelles are required to make this process possible?

_____

Benchmark Assessment SC.6.L.14.4

Fill in the letter of the best choice.

1 Rasheeda made a model of a plant cell and labeled parts of the cell that are **not** found in animal cells. Which other part of the cell should Rasheeda label?

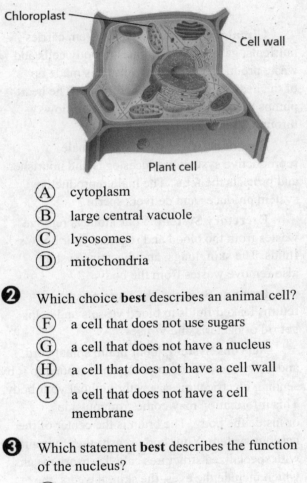

Plant cell

Ⓐ cytoplasm
Ⓑ large central vacuole
Ⓒ lysosomes
Ⓓ mitochondria

2 Which choice **best** describes an animal cell?

Ⓕ a cell that does not use sugars
Ⓖ a cell that does not have a nucleus
Ⓗ a cell that does not have a cell wall
Ⓘ a cell that does not have a cell membrane

3 Which statement **best** describes the function of the nucleus?

Ⓐ to hold a plant cell's DNA
Ⓑ to hold an animal cell's DNA
Ⓒ to hold all types of cells' DNA
Ⓓ to hold both plant and animal cells' DNA

4 Which is **true** of only animal cells?

Ⓕ Their cytoplasm contains organelles.
Ⓖ They do not have a rigid outermost layer.
Ⓗ The process of obtaining energy requires sugar.
Ⓘ They have organelles that are surrounded by membranes.

5 Ernest was looking at the following diagram of a cell. Which statement **best** explains how he should classify the cell?

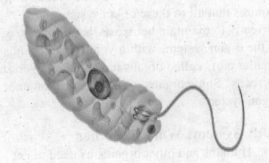

Ⓐ He should classify the cell as a plant cell because it has a cell membrane.
Ⓑ He should classify the cell as an animal cell because it has a flagellum.
Ⓒ He should classify the cell as a plant cell because it has cytoplasm.
Ⓓ He should not classify the cell as either a plant cell or an animal cell.

SC.6.L.14.5 Identify and investigate the general functions of the major systems of the human body (digestive, respiratory, circulatory, reproductive, excretory, immune, nervous, and musculoskeletal) and describe ways these systems interact with each other to maintain homeostasis.
SC.6.L.14.6 Compare and contrast types of infectious agents that may infect the human body, including viruses, bacteria, fungi, and parasites.

Human Body Systems

Systems in the Body

Our bodies are like incredibly complex machines. They can do some amazing things, but many parts must work together to make sure that they function properly. The human body is a system, meaning that it is made of a collection of parts that work together. In fact, the human body is a system made up of a collection of smaller systems, called organ systems. The human body requires that all of these organ systems work correctly to maintain homeostasis. Similarly, each of the organ systems within your body depends on smaller parts called organs to keep them working correctly. Some organs work in more than one organ system.

Body Systems Work Together

Humans and other organisms need to get energy. They need to use energy to run their bodies and move. They need to reproduce. They need to get rid of waste and protect their bodies. Organ systems help organisms to do all of these things. They also coordinate all the functions of a body. Organ systems in the human body include:

Digestive System: Your digestive system breaks down the food you eat into nutrients that can be used by the body. Chewing, a type of mechanical digestion, breaks down food into smaller pieces that are easier to swallow and digest. The stomach grinds food into a pulpy mixture. Nutrients are absorbed in the small intestine where most chemical digestion takes place.

Respiratory System: This system is responsible for gathering oxygen from the environment and gets ride of carbon dioxide from the body. This exchange happens in the lungs.

Circulatory System: This system carries nutrients, gases, and hormones to body cells and waste products from body cells. It is made up of the heart, blood vessels, and blood. The heart pumps blood through the body. Blood flows through blood vessels.

Reproductive System: The female reproductive system produces eggs and nourishes and protects the fetus. The male reproductive system produces and delivers sperm.

Excretory System: Your kidneys remove wastes from the blood and regulate your body's fluids. The skin, lungs, and digestive system also remove wastes from the body.

Immune System: The immune system returns leaked fluids to blood vessels and helps get rid of bacteria and viruses.

Nervous System: Your brain, spinal cord, and nerves collect information and respond to it by sending electrical messages throughout your body. This information may come from outside or inside the body. The brain is the center of the nervous system. Your body senses the environment with specialized structures called sensory organs, which include the eyes, the skin, the ears, the mouth, and the nose.

Musculoskeletal System: Your muscular system works with the skeletal system to help you move. Your skeletal system, which is made up of bones, ligaments, and cartilage, supports the body and protects important organs. It also makes blood cells.

Endocrine System: Your glands send out chemical messages. Ovaries and testes are part of this system.

The Endocrine System

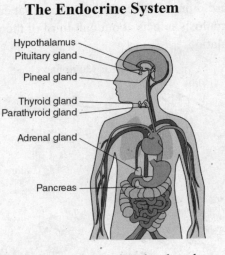

Hypothalamus
Pituitary gland
Pineal gland
Thyroid gland
Parathyroid gland
Adrenal gland
Pancreas

Our body systems can do a lot, but they cannot work alone! Almost everything we need for our bodies to work properly requires many body systems to work together. For example, the nervous system may sense danger. Nerves detect a stimulus in the environment and send a signal through the spinal cord to the brain. The brain sends a signal to respond. The endocrine system releases hormones that cause the heart to beat faster to deliver more oxygen through the circulatory system to muscles. The musculoskeletal system works to run away from danger.

Body Systems Communicate

In order to work together, body systems have to communicate. There are two basic ways they can communicate: by electrical messages and by chemical messages. Nerve cells transfer information between the body and the spinal cord and brain. Nerves pass electrical messages from one cell to the next along the line. The endocrine system sends chemical messages through the bloodstream to certain cells. Because chemicals are distinct from each other, cells, organs, and organ systems can respond to chemicals differently.

Homeostasis

Like cells, your body must maintain **homeostasis**, or the maintenance of a constant internal environment when outside conditions change. Your body needs to have the right

amounts of water, oxygen, nutrients, and warmth in order to function properly. Your body systems constantly work together to make sure these needs are being met.

If any body system fails to function properly, homeostasis may be disrupted. For example, a problem in the digestive system can cause the body to have a lack of nutrients. A lack of food harms many systems and may cause disease or even death. The presence of toxins or pathogens also can disrupt homeostasis. Toxins can prevent cells from carrying out life processes and pathogens can break down cells. Problems also occur if the body's messages do not work, or they are not sent when or where they are needed. Many diseases which affect homeostasis are hereditary.

Infection

Homeostasis in your body can be disrupted by harmful things in the environment. Microscopic organisms and particles, such as bacteria and viruses, are all around you. Most are harmless, but some can make you sick. Thankfully, our bodies have ways of protecting us against harmful agents such as these. Your skin provides external protection against pathogens that may enter the body. Most of the time, pathogens cannot get past external defenses. Sometimes, skin is cut and pathogens can enter the body. Your body may respond by raising your body temperature. This response is called fever, which slows the growth of bacteria and some other pathogens. If a pathogen is not destroyed by fever, then the immune system responds.

Noninfectious and Infectious Diseases

When you have a disease, your body does not function normally. Diseases cause specific symptoms, or changes in how a person feels. The many types of diseases can be categorized as either noninfectious or infectious.

Diseases that are caused by hereditary or environmental factors are called **noninfectious diseases**. For example, cystic fibrosis is caused by hereditary factors. People with cystic fibrosis inherited a mutated gene from each of their

Name_____ Date_____

parents. The gene causes excess mucus to build up in the lungs, pancreas, and other organs. This excess mucus can lead to infections and damage to organs. Other types of noninfectious diseases can be caused by environmental factors. Mutagens are environmental factors that cause mutations, or changes, in DNA. Sometimes, the changes cause a cell to reproduce uncontrollably. This results in a disease called cancer.

A disease that is caused by a pathogen is called an **infectious disease**. Pathogens include bacteria, fungi, and parasites, which are all alive. Pathogens also include viruses, which are non cellular particles that depend on living things to reproduce. Viruses are not considered to be alive because they cannot function on their own. A disease that spreads from person to person is a contagious disease. Diseases can be transmitted to people by other people, by other organisms and by contaminated food, water, or objects.

Types of Pathogens

Viruses are tiny particles that have their own genetic material but depend on living things to reproduce. Viruses insert their genetic material into a cell, and then the cell makes more viruses. The diagram shows how viruses destroy cells in the process of replicating themselves.

Bacteria are single-celled prokaryotic organisms. Most bacteria are beneficial to other living things. However, some bacteria cause

disease. For example, the bacterium that causes tuberculosis infects about one-third of the world's population.

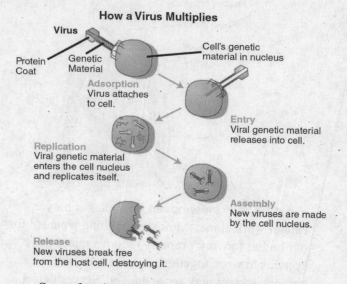

How a Virus Multiplies

Virus

Protein Coat
Genetic Material

Cell's genetic material in nucleus

Adsorption
Virus attaches to cell.

Entry
Viral genetic material releases into cell.

Replication
Viral genetic material enters the cell nucleus and replicates itself.

Assembly
New viruses are made by the cell nucleus.

Release
New viruses break free from the host cell, destroying it.

Some fungi are pathogens, but most fungi are beneficial. Fungi decompose, or break down, dead plants and animals into materials that other organisms use. A fungus that infects a living organism will damage the organism. The most common fungal diseases are skin infections.

A parasite is an organism that lives on and feeds on another organism, called a host. Parasites usually harm the host. Some of the most common parasites in humans are certain types of single-celled organisms called protists. For example, the protists that cause malaria infect as many as 500 million people each year.

Student-Response Activity

❶ What are four types of pathogens that can cause infectious disease?

_____

_____

_____

_____

❷ How are fungi and bacteria both similar to and different from one another? Answer by completing the Venn diagram.

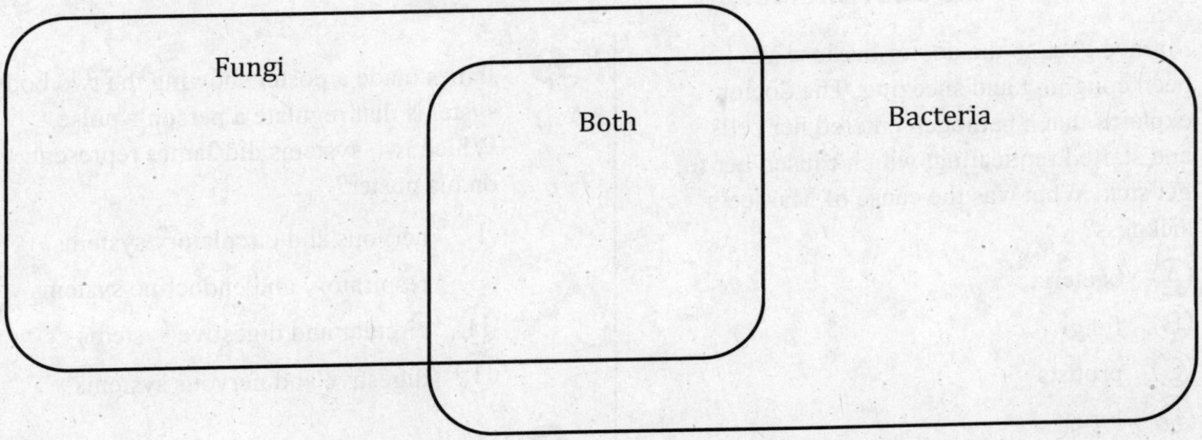

Fungi

Both

Bacteria

❸ All cells need oxygen to function properly. Which body systems need to coordinate to make sure cells receive oxygen?

_____

_____

❹ Jackie sees a tree branch about to fall on her, and she jumps out of the way. Which body systems helped her respond to danger?

_____

_____

❺ What is one example of an organ that is part of multiple body systems? Tell which body systems the organ is part of.

_____

_____

_____

❻ The stomach is part of the digestive system. Which other body systems would be affected if the stomach no longer functioned properly?

_____

_____

_____

Benchmark Assessment SC.6.L.14.5, SC.6.L.14.6

Fill in the letter of the best choice.

1 Marnee goes to the doctor because she has been coughing and sneezing. The doctor explains that a pathogen entered her cells and started replicating, which caused her to get sick. What was the cause of Marnee's sickness?

- (A) bacteria
- (B) fungi
- (C) protists
- (D) virus

2 The liver regulates how much sugar enters the bloodstream. What body systems is the liver a part of?

- (F) digestive and excretory systems
- (G) circulatory and digestive systems
- (H) respiratory and endocrine systems
- (I) musculoskeletal and integumentary systems

3 Kendrick made a model that included kidneys, liver, large intestine, and bladder. What is the **main** function of the body system that Kendrick built a model of?

- (A) It gets rid of wastes that the body produces.
- (B) It uses electrical signals to control body functions.
- (C) It uses chemical messages to control body functions.
- (D) It gets rid of pathogens that invade the body.

4 James made a poster showing the two body systems that regulate a person's pulse. Which two systems did James represent on his poster?

- (F) nervous and circulatory systems
- (G) respiratory and endocrine systems
- (H) circular and digestive systems
- (I) digestive and nervous systems

5 The endocrine system consists of many glands that produce chemical messages. These chemicals are sent to organs throughout the body. Which system works with the endocrine system to deliver the chemical messages to the body?

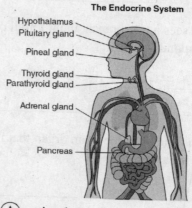

The Endocrine System

Hypothalamus
Pituitary gland
Pineal gland
Thyroid gland
Parathyroid gland
Adrenal gland
Pancreas

- (A) circulatory system
- (B) excretory system
- (C) nervous system
- (D) respiratory system

SC.6.L.15.1 Analyze and describe how and why organisms are classified according to shared characteristics with emphasis on the Linnaean system combined with the concept of Domains.

Classification of Living Things

The Tree of Life

There are millions of kinds of living things on Earth. How do scientists keep all of these living things organized? Scientists classify living things based on characteristics that living things share. Classification helps scientists answer questions such as:

- How many kinds of living things are there?
- What characteristics define each kind of living thing?
- What are the relationships among living things?

Scientists investigate these questions systematically. Using evidence gathered from many observations, scientists have developed hypotheses about how different living things are related. These hypotheses are often represented by a "tree of life" diagram. These diagrams, also called cladograms, show the relationships among organisms by a series of branching lines.

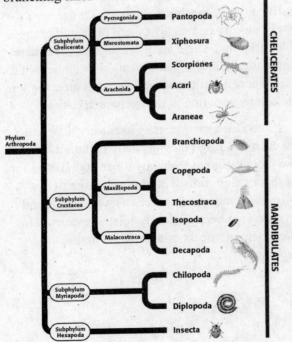

Scientists frequently debate how cladograms should be arranged, and new evidence frequently leads scientists to revise them. There is no one correct way to draw a tree of life, but they are still very useful. The cladogram here shows a hypothesis about how some arthropods are related.

Shared Characteristics

There are many animals on Earth that look similar. If two organisms look similar, are they related? Scientists have to look at many characteristics to decide whether or not two organisms are related. Scientists must compare physical characteristics, such as size or bone structure. Scientists also compare the chemical characteristics of living things.

Physical Characteristics

Scientists look at physical characteristics, such as skeletal structure. They also study how organisms develop from an egg to an adult. Organisms that have similar skeletons and development may be related. Kangaroos and mice, for instance, both have legs, hair, and a dorsal nerve cord, but the nature of development is different and their bipedal posture is different.

Chemical Characteristics

Scientists can identify the relationships among organisms by studying genetic material such as DNA and RNA. They use mutations and genetic similarities to find relationships among organisms. Organisms that have very similar gene sequences or have the same mutations are likely related. Other chemicals, such as proteins and hormones, can also be studied to learn how organisms are related.

Putting It All Together

The first scientist to systematically organize living things by their traits was a Swedish botanist named Carl Linnaeus. Linnaeus's ideas became the basis for modern taxonomy. **Taxonomy** is the science of describing, classifying, and naming living things. The way that scientists classify organisms today is based on the Linnaean system. The Linnaean system of classification is a hierarchy, or a system in which groups are put together and ranked. Linnaeus's original system had seven ranks. Linnaeus lived and worked in the 1700s. Since then, about 2 million new species have been described, and our understanding of the history of life has expanded greatly. As a result, the Linnaean system has had to expand as well. Today, scientists recognize many more levels above, between, and even below the original seven.

Below the level of kingdom, organisms are grouped into a phylum, class, order, family, genus, and species, as well as levels in between each of these.

Domains and Kingdoms

For Linnaeus, the kingdom was the highest level of organization. The highest rank in the modern system of classification is the domain. Carl Woese introduced domains. He realized that the previous kingdom system did not show similarities and differences between the eukaryotes and bacteria. A **domain** includes the greatest number of different organisms within it. All living things are grouped into one of three domains: Bacteria, Archae, and Eukarya. Human beings are in the domain Eukarya, along with fish, ferns, yeast, and amoebas, to name a few. The domain Bacteria is made up of prokaryotes that usually have a cell wall and reproduce by cell division. The domain Archae is also made up of prokaryotes, but they differ from bacteria in their genetics and the makeup of their cell walls. The domain Eukarya has cells with a nucleus and membrane-bound organelles.

The next rank below domain is kingdom. Eukarya has four kingdoms: Animalia, Plantae, Fungi, and Protista. Humans and fish are in the kingdom Animalia together. Ferns, yeasts, and amoebas are all in different kingdoms. That means that humans are more like fish than they are like amoebas, fungi, or plants.

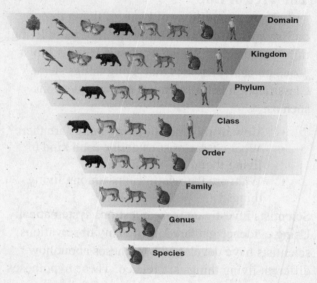

Genus and Species

Any organism that you can think of is a particular species. A species is the basic unit of classification. A **species** is a group of organisms that are very closely related. They can mate and produce fertile offspring. There are more species than there are any other levels of classification. Members of a species share all of the same characteristics, though there can be variation in those characteristics.

Lions, for example, may look very different from each other, but they all share certain traits that make them different from any other organism. Lions also share many traits with tigers, but the two species have many differences as well. Lions and tigers are members of closely related species. This makes them members of a common genus, *Panthera*.

A scientific name always includes the genus name followed by the specific name. The first letter of the genus name is capitalized, and the first letter of the specific name is lowercased. The entire scientific name is written either in italics or underlined. Consider the scientific name for a lion: *Panthera leo*. The first part, *Panthera*, is the genus name. A genus includes similar species. The second part, *leo*, is the specific, or species name. No other species is named *Panthera leo*.

Student-Response Activity

1 What are the eight main levels of classification from most general to most definite?

_____

_____

_____

_____

_____

_____

_____

2 Dr. Nick is describing a new species he discovered. He says it is large enough to see without a lens and it eats small plants. What domain and kingdom is the organism **most likely** in?

_____

_____

❸ Margaret tells her friends that she caught a fish called *Salmo salar*. What genus does the fish belong to? Explain how you know.

_____

_____

_____

_____

❹ A scientist finds a tiny fragment of a bone too small to be classified by its appearance. The scientist studies the tiny fragment and concludes that it belonged to an ancient primate species. How was the scientist able to classify the bone?

_____

_____

_____

_____

❺ Look at the diagram. Do both lemurs and humans have the traits listed at point D? Explain your reasoning.

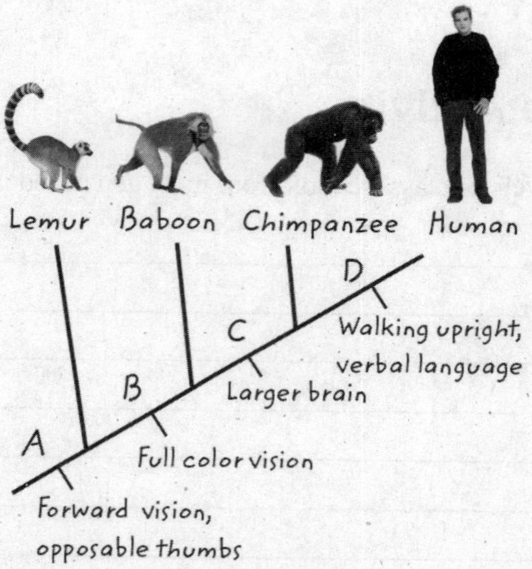

Lemur   Baboon   Chimpanzee   Human

D

Walking upright, verbal language

C

Larger brain

B

Full color vision

A

Forward vision, opposable thumbs

_____

_____

_____

_____

Benchmark Assessment SC.6.L.15.1

Fill in the letter of the best choice.

1 A scientist finds an organism that cannot move. It has many cells, produces spores, and gets food from its environment. In which kingdom does it belong?

   Ⓐ kingdom Animalia

   Ⓑ kingdom Fungi

   Ⓒ kingdom Plantae

   Ⓓ kingdom Protista

2 A student is building a model showing how living things are organized. Which pair of groups contains the greatest number of organisms?

   Ⓕ genus and species

   Ⓖ phylum and class

   Ⓗ domain and genus

   Ⓘ domain and kingdom

3 Two different kinds of organisms are as closely related as possible. Which statement is **most likely** true about the organisms?

   Ⓐ They are in the same genus.

   Ⓑ They are in the same species.

   Ⓒ They share the same DNA.

   Ⓓ They share no common ancestors.

4 Jessica learns that two organisms are members of the same class. Which can she also infer is **true**?

   Ⓕ The organisms are members of the same order.

   Ⓖ The organisms are members of the same family.

   Ⓗ The organisms are members of the same genus.

   Ⓘ The organisms are members of the same phylum.

5 Serena knows that scientists use physical characteristics to classify organisms. She studies the figures of four different organisms.

1   2   3   4

Which two organisms should Serena conclude are **most** closely related?

   Ⓐ 1 and 2

   Ⓑ 1 and 3

   Ⓒ 2 and 3

   Ⓓ 2 and 4

SC.7.L.15.1 Recognize that fossil evidence is consistent with the scientific theory of evolution that living things evolved from earlier species. **SC.7.L.15.2** Explore the scientific theory of evolution by recognizing and explaining ways in which genetic variation and environmental factors contribute to evolution by natural selection and diversity of organisms. **SC.7.L.15.3** Explore the scientific theory of evolution by relating how the inability of a species to adapt within in a changing environment may contribute to the extinction of the species.

Fossils and Evolution

Theory of Evolution by Natural Selection

Life first appeared on Earth nearly 4 billion years ago. The earliest life forms on Earth were very simple and very small. Over time organisms changed and became more and more complex. The process by which populations gradually change over time is called **evolution**. An early form of a species, called an *ancestor*, may give rise to many new *descendent* species over time. As populations change over time, new species form. Thus, newer species descend from older species. This idea is called the scientific theory of evolution.

The scientific theory of evolution explains how different species have appeared over time. The scientific theory of evolution by natural selection was first proposed in 1859, by Charles Darwin. **Natural selection** is the process by which organisms that inherit advantageous traits tend to reproduce more successfully than the other organisms do. There are four main parts of the natural selection process—overproduction, genetic variation, selection, and adaptation.

Mechanisms of Natural Selection

Overproduction occurs when more organisms are born than can survive in the environment. A fish, for example, may produce thousands of eggs, but only a few of them will be likely to survive and reproduce.

Within a species there are natural variations, or differences in traits. Genetic variations can be passed on from parent to offspring. Sometimes a mutation takes place and changes genetic material.

With each new generation, new genetic variations may be introduced into a population. The more genetic variation a population has, the more likely it is that some individuals might have traits that will be advantageous if the environment changes.

Selection happens when organisms with certain traits are more likely to survive long enough to reproduce. Some organisms in a population may have traits that help them survive in a particular environment. These organisms are most likely to survive to pass on their genes to the next generation. The next generation will have the same traits that helped the previous generation survive. If the environment changes, the genes and traits that help organisms survive may change as well. When this happens, the trait has been "selected" or becomes more common in the next generation of offspring.

Adaptations are genetic variations that help a species survive and reproduce in a particular environment. Some adaptations, such as the bird beaks and feet shown on the next page, are physical. Other adaptations can be behaviors that help an organism find food, protect itself, or reproduce. Over time, adaptations that help organisms survive spread through a population. When this happens, populations are better able to survive.

Beak and Feet Adaptations			
Type of beak	Adapted for	Type of foot	Adapted for
	eating seeds		perching
	eating insects		wading
	probing for food		preying
	preying on animals		swimming
	straining food from water		climbing
	eating fish		

Extinction

What happens when an environment changes after a species has adapted to it? The environmental change could be gradual, or it could happen suddenly. Changes in environmental conditions can affect the survival of individuals with a particular trait. At first, the species may be able to survive. But, if no individuals are born with traits that help them survive and reproduce in the changed environment, the species will become extinct. **Extinction** is when all the members of a species have died. Competition, new predators, and the loss of habitat are environmental pressures that can limit the growth of populations and could lead to extinction.

Fossil Record

Scientists accept the theory of evolution because it is supported by evidence. Some of the evidence is found in fossils. Millions of years ago, life in Florida was very different than it is today. We know this because millions of years ago living things left behind fossils. **Fossils** are the mineralized remains or imprints of organisms that lived long ago. All the fossils that have been discovered make up the **fossil record**.

In Florida, all fossils older than 25 million years are marine fossils, because Florida was completely covered by ocean water. These fossils include shells, corals, sea urchins, sharks, sea turtles, and a whale. In Florida, fossils of land animals found in rocks and sediments date back to about 25 million years ago. The fossil record indicates that most of these land animals became extinct in Florida about 10,000 years ago.

Many fossils that people find are from extinct species. While no members of an extinct species can be found alive, many extinct species are very similar to organisms that are alive today. Scientists have concluded that these extinct organisms are related to similar living ones. Their conclusions are consistent with the scientific theory of evolution.

Living Records

Many scientific fields of study provide evidence that modern species and extinct species share an ancestor. A *common ancestor* is the most recent species from which two different species have evolved.

Modern Whale Skeleton

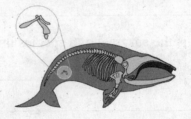

Scientists have found that organisms that are related also share structural traits. Structures in today's organisms that may be reduced in size or in function may have been complete and functional in the organism's ancestor. For example, scientists studied the characteristics of whales that made them different from other ocean animals. Unlike fish and sharks, whales breathe air, give birth to live young, and produce milk. Scientists have examined fossils of extinct species with features in between whales and land mammals. These features are called transitional characters. The DNA of whales is very similar to the DNA of hoofed mammals. Some whales have tiny hip bones left over from their hoofed-mammal ancestors, like those shown above. Evidence collected from fossils, DNA, and structures support the hypothesis that modern whales evolved from hoofed mammals that lived on land.

Student-Response Activity

1 Describe how each adaptation helps the species survive and/or reproduce.

Organism	Adaptation	Role in Survival or Reproduction
Venus flytrap	trap helps catch prey	
frog	skin looks like a dead leaf	
bird	male has large red throat pouch	
butterfly	long tongue to reach inside flower	

2 How can natural selection account for the long tongues of butterflies?

_____

_____

3 How is the survival of a species impacted by the environment?

_____

_____

4 What are two ways a fish is adapted to its environment?

_____

_____

_____

5 Suppose you are a scientist examining the DNA sequence of two unknown organisms that you hypothesize share a common ancestor. What evidence would you expect to find?

_____

_____

_____

6 What are two types of evidence that suggest evolution has occurred?

_____

_____

_____

Benchmark Assessment SC.7.L.15.1, SC.7.L.15.2, SC.7.L.15.3

Fill in the letter of the best choice.

 1 A scientist observes that the leg bones of cats are similar to the bones in the wings of bats. The scientist concludes the two species share a common ancestor. Which describes why the scientist drew that conclusion?

(A) developmental patterns

(B) DNA

(C) fossil evidence

(D) structural data

2 Bald eagles might lay up to five eggs at a time, but only one hatchling usually survives. Which feature of natural selection is this an example of?

(F) adaptation

(G) genetic variation

(H) overproduction

(I) selection

3 The scientific theory of evolution is accepted by scientists as a way to explain the diversity of life on Earth. Which **best** describes the process of evolution?

(A) Populations gradually change over time.

(B) Populations change rapidly and then go extinct.

(C) Populations go extinct and new species take their place.

(D) Populations change into new species when the environment changes.

4 This fossil is of a species that no longer exists on Earth.

What is this fossil evidence of?

(F) evolution

(G) extinction

(H) natural selection

(I) overproduction

5 Snowshoe hares live in areas with cool summers and extreme winters. In the summer, their fur is brown. In the winter, they grow white fur. Which **best** describes what this is an example of?

(A) adaptation

(B) evolution

(C) selection

(D) variation

SC.7.L.16.1 Understand and explain that every organism requires a set of instructions that specifies its traits, that this hereditary information (DNA) contains genes located in the chromosomes of each cell, and that heredity is the passage of these instructions from one generation to another. **SC.7.L.16.2** Determine the probabilities for genotype and phenotype combinations using Punnett squares and pedigrees. **SC.7.L.16.3** Compare and contrast the general processes of sexual reproduction requiring meiosis and asexual reproduction requiring mitosis.

Reproduction and Heredity

From Genes to Organisms

Every organism, from single-celled bacteria to giant sequoia trees, is made out of cells. Every cell within an organism contains all of the instructions the organism needs to grow and survive! The information in cells is stored in a special molecule called **DNA**. DNA contains sections called **genes** that tell cells how to build proteins. In this way, cells can build all of the structures the organism needs to survive.

Cell Division

The life cycle of an organism includes birth, growth, reproduction, and death. The life cycle of a eukaryotic cell, called the cell cycle, can be divided into three stages: interphase, mitosis, and cytokinesis. During the cell cycle, a parent cell divides into two new cells, called daughter cells. The new cells are identical to the parent.

Cells need to reproduce to ensure that the instructions carried in their DNA can survive. Cells reproduce themselves through a process called cell division. Cell division happens in all organisms and takes place for different reasons. For example, single-celled organisms reproduce through cell division. In multicellular organisms, cell division is involved in growth, development, and repair, as well as reproduction.

During most of a cell's life cycle, DNA is wrapped around special proteins in a complex material called **chromatin**. Before cell division, DNA is duplicated, or copied. Then, in an early stage of cell division, the chromatin is compacted into visible structures called chromosomes. A duplicated chromosome consists of two identical structures called **chromatids**. The chromatids of eukaryotic cells are held together by a **centromere**.

After all the DNA has been duplicated, the cell can divide into two new cells. This process is called **mitosis** in eukaryotic cells. Prokaryotic cells undergo a similar process called binary fission.

Mitosis

Meiosis

Most eukaryotic organisms reproduce by sexual reproduction. Sexual reproduction requires organisms to make specialized cells called gametes. Male gametes are called sperm cells, and female gametes are called egg cells. Gametes are different from all other cells in the body because they contain only a single copy of each chromosome, while body cells contain pairs of each. For example, humans have 46 chromosomes in each body cell, or 23 pairs. Human gametes have only 23 total chromosomes each. Cells with two copies of each chromosome are called **diploid** cells. Those with just one copy are called **haploid** cells.

Because gametes are different from other body cells, they require a special process to make them. The process of cell division that forms gametes is called **meiosis**. Meiosis is similar to mitosis, but each daughter cell goes through an extra round of cell division. A single cell undergoing meiosis will result in four daughter cells with a single copy of each chromosome instead of two daughter cells with two copies each.

Meiosis

Heredity

When two gametes combine to form a new organism, all of the cells of the new organism will again have two copies of each chromosome. One copy of each chromosome will have come from either parent. The new organism will then have traits similar to each parent. The passing on of information from parents to offspring is called **heredity**.

About 150 years ago, Gregor Mendel discovered the principles of heredity while studying pea plants. Mendel knew from his experiments with plants that there must be two sets of instructions for each trait an organism inherits. Scientists now call these instructions for inherited traits **genes**. Each parent gives one set of genes to the offspring. The offspring then has two forms of the same gene for every characteristic, or feature—one from each parent.

The different forms of a gene are called **alleles**. Many alleles are either dominant or recessive. If an allele is dominant, then the trait it encodes will be the one that shows up. For example, consider the gene responsible for producing dimples, or creases in the cheeks. This gene comes in two alleles: one for dimples and one for no dimples. If you have even one copy of the

allele for dimples, you will have dimples. This happens because the allele for producing dimples is dominant. An organism needs to receive two copies of a recessive gene to have the recessive trait.

Punnett Squares and Pedigrees

When Gregor Mendel studied pea plants, he noticed that traits are inherited in patterns. One tool for understanding the patterns of heredity is a diagram called a **Punnett square**. A Punnett square is a graphic used to predict the possible genotypes of offspring in a given cross. Each parent has two alleles for a particular gene. An offspring receives one allele from each parent. A Punnett square shows all of the possible allele combinations in the offspring.

In the Punnett square below, the letter *h* represents a gene with two alleles. The capital *H* represents the dominant allele, and the lowercase *h* represents the recessive allele. Because each parent has two alleles, but only contributes one to their offspring, different combinations are possible. The Punnett square shows all possible combinations.

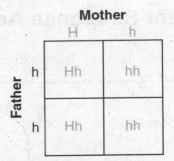

A Punnett square does not tell you what the exact results of a certain cross will be. A Punnett square only helps you find the probability that a certain genotype will occur. **Probability** is the mathematical chance of a specific outcome in relation to the total number of possible outcomes. Probability can be expressed in the form of a **ratio**, which is an expression that compares two quantities. A ratio written as 1:4 is read as "one to four." The ratios obtained from a Punnett square tell you the probability that any one offspring will get certain alleles.

Another way of expressing probability is as a percentage. A percentage is like a ratio that compares a number to 100. A percentage states the number of times a certain outcome might happen out of a hundred chances.

A pedigree is another tool used to study patterns of inheritance. A **pedigree** traces the occurrence of a trait through generations of a family. Pedigrees can trace any inherited trait—such as hair color. Squares in a pedigree represent males, and circles represent females. A horizontal line between a square and a circle represents a pair of parents. Vertical lines down connect parents to offspring.

The pedigree to the right traces eye shape in a family across four generations. Eyes can be either round or almond-shaped. The allele for almond-shaped eyes is dominant to the allele for

round eyes. People who have two different alleles are shown in the pedigree by a square or circle that is half shaded. Individuals with two different alleles of a gene are **heterozygous** for that gene. If a child is heterozygous for the recessive allele, then the child will have almond-shaped eyes. Individuals with two identical copies of a single gene are **homozygous** for that gene. People with two copies of the recessive allele are shown by a fully shaded square or circle. These offspring will have round eyes. Many other traits follow a similar pattern.

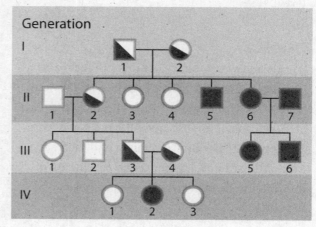

Student-Response Activity

❶ Complete the Venn diagram to compare and contrast the processes of mitosis and meiosis.

Mitosis

Both

Meiosis

② How many individuals in this pedigree are homozygous, and how many are heterozygous?

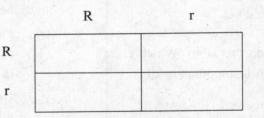

_____

_____

_____

_____

③ The Punnett square shows a cross between two fruit flies. The allele "R" gives red eyes, and the allele "r" gives white eyes. The "R" allele is dominant to the "r" allele. Which trait will each combination of alleles give? Fill in your answers on the Punnett square.

	R	r
R		
r		

④ What is the probability that an offspring from the cross above will have the allele combinations shown below? Write your answer as a percentage.

RR _____

Rr _____

rr _____

⑤ One thing that all cells have in common is they all contain the molecule DNA. Why do all cells have DNA?

_____

_____

_____

Name_____ Date _____

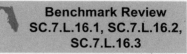

Benchmark Assessment SC.7.L.16.1, SC.7.L.16.2, SC.7.L.16.3

Fill in the letter of the best choice.

1 Cassie draws flashcards for each phase of mitosis and cytokinesis. Before she can label the backs of the flashcards, Cassie drops them onto the floor. The flashcards get mixed up as shown below.

In what order should Cassie place the cards to show mitosis from start to finish?

(A) $1 \rightarrow 2 \rightarrow 3 \rightarrow 4 \rightarrow 5$

(B) $2 \rightarrow 4 \rightarrow 5 \rightarrow 1 \rightarrow 3$

(C) $3 \rightarrow 1 \rightarrow 5 \rightarrow 2 \rightarrow 4$

(D) $4 \rightarrow 2 \rightarrow 1 \rightarrow 5 \rightarrow 3$

2 All cells contain the molecule DNA. Which **best** explains why DNA is important to all cells?

(F) All cells need DNA to process sugars.

(G) All cells need DNA to carry information.

(H) All cells need DNA to reproduce asexually.

(I) All cells need DNA to perform photosynthesis.

3 A bacterial cell divides to produce a new cell. Which **best** describes this?

(A) asexual reproduction

(B) meiosis

(C) mitosis

(D) sexual reproduction

4 In pea plants, the allele which produces yellow peas, Y, is dominant to the allele which produces green peas, y. Two pea plants with yellow peas are crossed and produce some offspring that produce green peas. Which **best** explains why?

(F) The parent plants were homozygous for the Y allele.

(G) The parent plants were heterozygous for the Y allele.

(H) The parent plants were homozygous for the y allele.

(I) The parent plants were homozygous for both alleles.

5 Heredity is the passage of information from one generation to the next. Which **best** describes heredity in sexual reproduction?

(A) Parents pass on DNA through mitosis.

(B) Genes are reproduced and recombined in meiosis.

(C) Gametes formed in meiosis fuse to make a new organism.

(D) Offspring acquire chromosomes from parents through binary fission.

6 The Punnett square shows the possible outcomes for a cross between two parents.

	S	s
S	SS	Ss
s	Ss	ss

The genotype of one parent is shown. What is the genotype of the other parent?

(F) S

(G) s

(H) Ss

(I) ss

SC.7.L.17.1 Explain and illustrate the roles of and relationships among producers, consumers, and decomposers in the process of energy transfer in a food web. **SC.7.L.17.2** Compare and contrast the relationships among organisms, such as mutualism, predation, parasitism, competition, and commensalism. **SC.7.L.17.3** Describe and investigate various limiting factors in the local ecosystem and their impact on native populations, including food, shelter, water, space, disease, parasitism, predation, and nesting sites.

Energy Transfer in a Food Web

Feeding Roles in an Ecosystem

All living things need a source of chemical energy to survive. Chemical energy is stored in the bonds of molecules. The energy stored in food is chemical energy in the bonds of food molecules. How an organism gets that chemical energy largely defines its role in the ecosystem.

Food Webs

Energy is all around us. All living things need a source of chemical energy to survive. A **producer** uses energy to make food. Most producers use sunlight to make food in a process called photosynthesis. Many producers are plants, but algae and some bacteria are also producers. Algae are the main producers in the ocean. The food that producers make supplies the energy for other living things.

Organisms that eat other organisms are called **consumers**. Consumers eat producers or other animals to obtain energy because they cannot make their own food. A consumer that eats only plants is called an **herbivore**. A **carnivore** is a consumer that eats animals. An **omnivore** eats both plants and animals. Scavengers are omnivores that eat dead plants and animals. Organisms that get energy by breaking down dead organisms are called **decomposers**.

Bacteria and fungi are decomposers. These organisms remove stored energy from dead organisms. They produce simple materials, such as water and carbon dioxide, which can be used by other living things. Decomposers are nature's recyclers. By converting dead organisms and animal and plant waste into materials such as water and nutrients, decomposers help move matter through ecosystems.

Organisms change energy from the environment or from their food into other types of energy. Some energy is used for the organism's activities, such as breathing or moving. Some energy is saved within the organism to use later. If an organism is eaten or decomposes, the consumer or decomposer takes in the energy stored in the original organism. Only chemical energy that an organism has stored in its tissues is available to consumers. In this way, energy is transferred from organism to organism.

A **food chain** is the path of energy transfer from producers to consumers. Energy moves from one organism to the next in one direction. The arrows in a food chain represent the transfer of energy, as one organism is eaten by another. Arrows represent the flow of energy from the body of the consumed organism to the body of the consumer of that organism. Producers form the base of food chains. Producers transfer energy to the first, or primary, consumer in the food chain. The next, or secondary, consumer in the food chain consumes the primary consumer. A tertiary consumer eats the secondary consumer. Finally, decomposers recycle matter back to the soil.

**Benchmark Review
SC.7.L.17.1, SC.7.L.17.2,
SC.7.L.17.3**

Few organisms eat just one kind of food. So, the energy and nutrient connections in nature are more complicated than a simple food chain. A **food web** is the feeding relationships among organisms in an ecosystem. Food webs are made up of many food chains.

Food Web

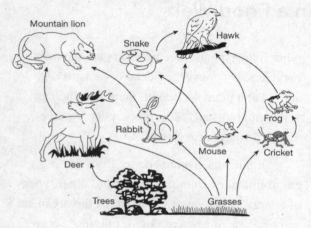

Relationships Among Organisms

Many organisms in nature form associations with each other. Such a relationship is called **symbiosis**. Symbiotic relationships are always beneficial to at least one organism, but may not be for the other. Often, one organism lives in or on the other organism. Symbiotic relationships are classified as mutualism, commensalism, or parasitism.

A symbiotic relationship in which both organisms benefit is called **mutualism**. An example of this is the relationship between bees and flowers. The bees gather nectar from the flower and while doing so, pollen attaches to their bodies. They transport this pollen to other flowers, which pollinates them. Without bees some types of plants would not get pollinated. Neither organism was harmed in this relationship.

A relationship between two organisms in which one benefits and the other is unaffected is called **commensalism**. An example of this is barnacles that attach to scallop shells. The barnacles gain a place to live while not harming or helping the scallop. Some examples of commensalism involve protection. For example, certain shrimp live among the spines of the fire urchin. The fire urchin's spines are poisonous but not to the shrimp. By living among the urchin's spines, the shrimp are protected from predators. In this relationship, the shrimp benefits and the fire urchin is unaffected.

A symbiotic association in which one organism benefits while the other is harmed is called **parasitism.** The organism that benefits is called the parasite. The organism that is harmed is called the host. The parasite gets nourishment from its host while the host is weakened. Sometimes, a host dies. Parasites, such as ticks, live outside the host's body. Other parasites, such as tapeworms, live inside the host's body.

Predation

Every organism lives with and affects other organisms. Many organisms must feed on other organisms to get the energy and nutrients they need to survive. These feeding relationships establish structure within a community.

Many interactions between species consist of one organism eating another. An animal that is eaten is called the **prey**. The organism that eats the prey is called the **predator**. When a bird eats a worm, the worm is prey, and the bird is the predator.

Competition

In a biological community, organisms compete for resources. Competition occurs when organisms fight for the same limited resource. Sometimes competition happens among individuals of the same species. For example, different groups of lions compete with each other for living space. Males within these groups also compete with each other for mates.

Competition can also happen among individuals of different species. Plants have to compete with each other for access to light, water, and space. If a forest is crowded with many trees, smaller plants may have a hard time getting sunlight.

Limiting factors

Populations cannot grow without stopping, because the environment contains a limited amount of food, water, living space, and other resources. Because there is a limited amount of resources in any ecosystem, communities of organisms are in competition with each other. Animals that eat the same foods compete for food resources. Animals may also compete for territory or access to mates. Having enough space to

spread out also helps prevent the spread of disease and parasites in a community. Disease and parasites can also act as limiting factors by reducing survival rates in a community.

A **limiting factor** is an environmental factor that keeps a population from reaching its full potential size. For example, food becomes a limiting factor when a population becomes too large for the amount of food available. Any single resource can be a limiting factor to a population's size. The largest population that an environment can support is known as the carrying capacity. When a population grows larger than its carrying capacity, limiting factors in the environment cause individuals to die off or leave. As individuals die or leave, the population decreases.

One factor limits a population at a time. Suppose the area that had only enough food for 500 armadillos suddenly had enough food for 2,000 armadillos, but only enough water for 1,000 armadillos. The population still could not grow to 2,000 armadillos. Water would keep the population at 1,000 armadillos. In this case, water is the limiting factor.

Student-Response Activity

❶ A rhinoceros feeds mainly on grasses. Ticks climb onto a rhinoceros to feed on its blood. Tick birds land on the rhinoceros to feed on the ticks. What are the two types of symbiosis being described, and which organisms form each symbiotic relationship?

_____

_____

_____

_____

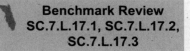
❷ Look at the food web diagram.

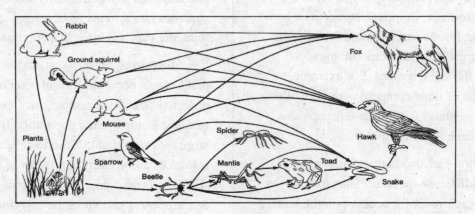

What is one way that energy from the sun provides energy for the hawk? Describe the role of each
organism involved in the process.

_____
_____
_____
_____

❸ How does the environment limit what organisms can survive in an area? Give at least one example.

_____
_____
_____

❹ How might carnivores be affected if the main plant species in a community were to disappear?

_____
_____
_____
_____

❺ What are two ways that plants compete with one another?

_____
_____
_____
_____

Benchmark Assessment SC.7.L.17.1, SC.7.L.17.2, SC.7.L.17.3

Fill in the letter of the best choice.

1 Look at the food web diagram.

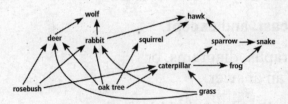

Which **best** describes a relationship shown in the food web?

(A) Wolves are symbiotic with hawks.

(B) Squirrels are predators of hawks.

(C) Caterpillars are decomposers of grass.

(D) Deer are in competition with squirrels.

2 Symbiosis occurs when two organisms form an association. Symbiotic relationships can be commensal, mutualistic, or parasitic. Which **best** describes a commensal relationship?

(F) Remoras attach to sharks in order to eat scraps the shark does not eat. The sharks are unharmed.

(G) A tick attaches to an impala in order to feed on its blood. The tick benefits while the impala is harmed.

(H) A lichen is an organism formed by a fungus and a bacteria working together. Both the fungus and the bacteria benefit.

(I) Brown-headed cowbirds lay their eggs in the nests of other birds. The cowbird benefits while the other bird species is harmed.

3 Which **best** describes a producer?

(A) A squirrel stores acorns away to eat in the winter.

(B) A vulture eats the decomposing carcass of a deer.

(C) A pine tree absorbs matter and converts it to food.

(D) Fungi absorb nutrients directly from the environment.

4 Look at the food web diagram.

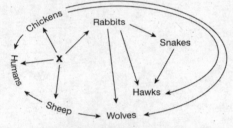

Which **most likely** represents the X?

(F) corn

(G) eggs

(H) foxes

(I) worms

5 Devon noticed that it has rained more this year than it did in each of the previous 10 years. How might this affect populations in the area?

(A) Populations for whom water is a limiting factor will decrease in size.

(B) Populations for whom water is a limiting factor will increase in size.

(C) Populations for whom water is not a limiting factor will decrease in size.

(D) Populations for whom water is not a limiting factor will increase in size.

FSSA Practice Test–Form A

Instructions–Form A

The following pages contain a practice test. Do not look at the test until your teacher tells you to begin.

Use the answer sheet on page 125 to mark your answers.

Read each question carefully. Restate the question in your own words.

Watch for key words such as **best, not, most, least,** and **except**.

A question might include one or more tables, graphs, diagrams, or pictures. Study these carefully before choosing an answer.

For questions 1–40, find the best answer. Fill in the answer bubble for that answer. Do not make any stray marks around answer spaces.

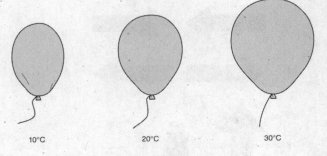

1 The diagram below shows Neils Bohr's theory about how electrons are arranged in atoms. He thought electrons traveled on specific paths around a nucleus. The current theory is that electrons exist in certain cloudlike regions around a nucleus.

Atom

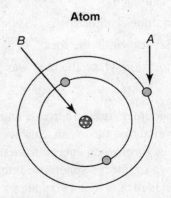

How would a model of the current theory differ from Bohr's model?

A Both objects A and B would differ from Bohr's model.

B It would be the same as Bohr's model.

C Object A would differ from Bohr's model.

D Object B would differ from Bohr's model.

2 Bryan recorded the mass of a kitten in the table below. What would be the best scale to use for the mass variable when making a line graph of the data shown?

Growth of a Kitten	
Age (weeks)	Mass (g)
6	2,560
7	2,790
8	2,850
9	2,920
10	3,120

F 0 to 2,500 in units of 10

G 0 to 2,500 in units of 500

H 2,500 to 3,500 in units of 50

I 2,000 to 3,000 in units of 100

3 A physicist at a research laboratory reports a startling new discovery. However, other scientists are unable to reproduce the results of the experiment. Which is the **most likely** explanation for the faulty results?

A The results are announced to the public.

B The conclusions are based on multiple trials.

C The data collection was not accurate or precise.

D Other scientists do not have as sophisticated equipment.

4 Steve uses balloons to investigate the expansion and contraction of gases at different temperatures. He knows that particles move faster at higher temperatures. He develops the hypothesis that faster particle motion makes gases expand. He fills three balloons with the same amount of gas. The independent variable is the temperature of the gas. Based on the figure below, which describes how the dependent variable changes as a result of the manipulation of the independent variable?

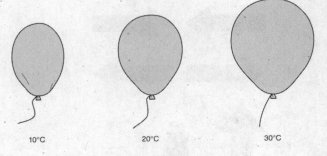

10°C   20°C   30°C

F The number of gas particles increases at higher temperatures.

G The number of gas particles decreases at higher temperatures.

H Gas particles move faster and farther apart at higher temperatures.

I Gas particles move more slowly and get closer together at higher temperatures.

5 Kathleen made the diagram below to show how scientific knowledge changes over time. Which **best** describes what scientists would do at the point indicated by the blank?

Original idea + new data → __?__ → modified idea

A debate the change

B change the data

C propose a law

D form an opinion

6 Earth's core is composed of two separate layers–the inner core and the outer core. What is one difference between these two layers?

F One is iron, and one is nickel.

G One is iron, and one is zinc.

H One is liquid, and one is gas.

I One is solid, and one is liquid.

7 Volcanoes often form at convergent plate boundaries. Which represents a convergent plate boundary?

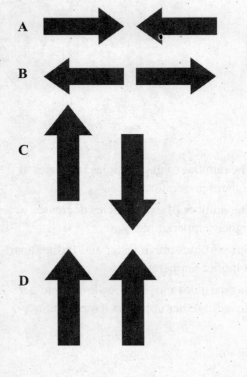

A

B

C

D

8 Declan observed a rock that he found at the beach. The rock felt hard, it was yellow, and it appeared to be made of layers. Declan concluded that the rock was sedimentary. Which **best** supports this conclusion?

F the yellow color

G the hardness of the rock

H the layers within the rock

I the location where the rock was found

9 Ships encounter surface currents and waves as they travel across the ocean. Surface currents and waves form when energy from the sun causes two of Earth's spheres to interact. Based on this evidence, which two spheres interact to produce these waves and currents?

A the geosphere and biosphere

B the biosphere and hydrosphere

C the cryosphere and atmosphere

D the atmosphere and hydrosphere

10 The town of Winchester recently built an artificial body of water. This reservoir, shown below, will store drinking water for the town.

Which could cause contamination of the water and lead to health-related problems?

F a water treatment facility

G increase in fertilizer use

H use of nontoxic chemicals

I water stewardship

11 A team of scientists is searching for specimens to understand how Earth's climate has changed in the past. The black boxes in the figure below show where this team has drilled to obtain such specimens.

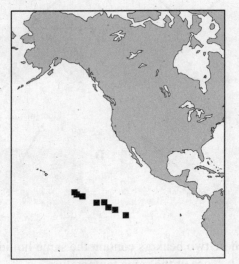

What were these scientists drilling for?

A ice cores

B surface landforms

C sea-floor sediments

D fossils preserved in amber

12 Which **best** describes how the sun causes wind?

F The sun heats Earth unevenly, causing warm air to rise and cool air to sink, which causes differences in air pressure.

G The sun heats Earth evenly, which causes all air to rise.

H The sun heats Earth unevenly, causing warm air to sink and cool air to rise, which causes differences in air pressure.

I The sun heats Earth evenly, which causes all air to sink.

13 A trace fossil includes no physical remains of the organism's body, but only a mark or structure that the organism left behind. Which is **not** an example of a trace fossil?

A burrow in the sea floor

B coprolite in sediment

C footprint in sediment

D insect in amber

14 One ball rolls along a shelf at a steady rate. A second ball rolls off the shelf and gains speed as it falls in a curved path. Which ball must have an unbalanced force acting on it?

F both balls

G neither ball

H the ball that falls

I the ball that rolls along the shelf

15 The diagram below shows a wave. The features of the wave are labeled A, B, C, and D.

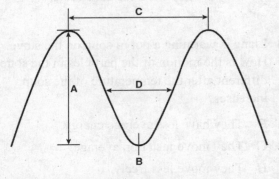

Which identifies the wavelength?

A A

B B

C C

D D

16 Jeanine looks around her classroom at different objects. Which reflects almost all of the light that strikes it?

   F white poster board

   G clear window glass

   H bright overhead light

   I black construction paper

17 Sonia tapped one end of a long wooden table. Sanjay and Marc listened for the sounds. Sanjay pressed his ear to the table and heard the taps that seemed louder than the taps that Marc heard. Why?

   A More energy reached Sanjay's ear than Marc's ear.

   B Particles of wood are farther apart than particles of air.

   C Sound travels through air and wood at different speeds.

   D The taps only made the table vibrate, they did not make the air vibrate.

18 Liang is warming a pot of soup on the stove. How is the motion of the particles in the soup different after the temperature of the soup increases?

   F They have less average energy.

   G They move faster on average.

   H They move less freely.

   I They vibrate and are close together.

19 Calvin shines a thin beam of light onto a material, and the light refracts. Which **best** shows what happens to the light?

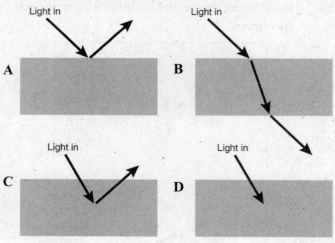

20 These two beakers contain the same liquid substance at the same temperature.

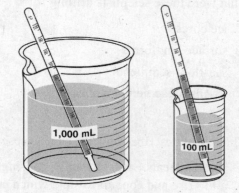

How does the thermal energy of the liquid in the larger beaker compare or contrast with the thermal energy of the liquid in the smaller beaker?

   F The liquid in the larger beaker has less thermal energy than the liquid in the smaller beaker.

   G The liquid in the larger beaker has more thermal energy than the liquid in the smaller beaker.

   H The liquid in the larger beaker has the same amount of thermal energy as the liquid in the smaller beaker.

   I The exact volume of liquid in each beaker must be known to compare the thermal energy of the liquids.

21 Luis is trying to push a box of new soccer balls across the floor. In the illustration below, the arrow on the box represents the force that Luis exerts.

If the box is not moving, which must be **true**?

A Luis is applying a force that acts at a distance.

B The box is exerting a larger force on Luis than he is exerting on the box.

C There is another force acting on the box that balances Luis's force.

D There is no force of friction acting on the box.

22 Damon is a musician playing in a band. At the end of a song, he plucks a single guitar string. The string moves rapidly back and forth as shown in the figure below.

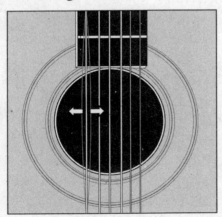

Which explains what happens to the kinetic energy of the moving string?

F The kinetic energy is changed into potential energy and stored.

G The kinetic energy is slowly destroyed until no energy remains.

H The kinetic energy is converted to sound energy and thermal energy.

I Some of the energy is converted to sound energy, but the rest is destroyed.

23 While exploring a rock formation, Hiroto finds a rock that has footprints pressed into it. A geologist tells Hiroto that the rock is millions of years old. Which is **correct** about Hiroto's find?

A It is not a fossil, because footprints are not fossils.

B It is not a fossil, because only whole organisms are fossils.

C It is a fossil only if Hiroto finds actual parts of the organism in rocks nearby.

D It is a fossil because footprints of organisms from millions of years ago are considered to be fossils.

24 Mammals are complex organisms whose bodies are highly organized. Which lists levels of organization in mammals from **least** organized to **most** organized?

F cells → molecules → atoms

G cells → tissues → organs

H molecules → tissues → cells

I organs → tissues → cells

25 A species of rodent lives in a moist forest. Over time, the climate becomes drier and more desert-like. Which adaptation is **most likely** to improve the chances that the species will survive as its environment changes?

A having dark hair and small ears

B living above ground in damp areas

C being able to eat only one type of berry

D being able to eat plants that survive in the changed environment

26 Charles Darwin observed differences in the shapes of the birds' beaks on the Galápagos Islands. Finches that ate insects had longer, narrower beaks than finches that crushed and ate seeds. Which finch is **most likely** adapted to eating seeds?

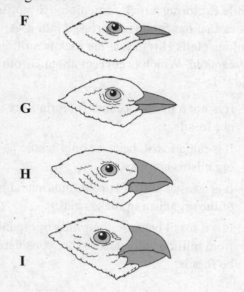

F

G

H

I

27 Delia is teaching her sister about important molecules in the body. She tells her sister that one molecule provides a set of instructions that determines characteristics, such as eye color or hair color. Which is Delia describing?

A DNA

B glucose

C gamete

D spore

28 Examine the Punnett square below. The alleles of one parent are Ss.

	S	s
S	SS	Ss
s	Ss	ss

Which are the alleles of the second parent?

F SS

G Ss

H ss

I Sr

29 One part of the cell theory states that cells come from other cells. Which statement **best** explains that this part of the cell theory applies to all organisms?

A The cells of all organisms excrete waste.

B The cells of all organisms have cytoplasm.

C The cells of all organisms divide to make more cells.

D The cells of all organisms take in nutrients from their environment.

30 Which correctly pairs a type of cell with how it could be produced?

F egg cell—meiosis in males

G sperm cell—mitosis in males

H body cell—mitosis in females

I body cell—meiosis in females

31 Mangrove swamps are found along the southern coasts of Florida. A mangrove swamp contains an ecosystem of many organisms living among the large roots of the mangrove trees. This food web shows some of the relationships in that ecosystem.

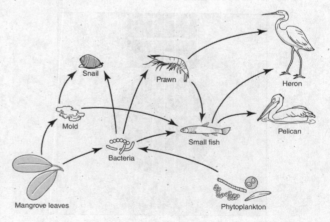

Which is a producer in the mangrove swamp?

A bacteria

B heron

C mold

D phytoplankton

32 The interiors of some plants have tunnels and holes that ants can live in. These plants may also produce food on their leaves that ants like to eat. Which is **not likely** a reason that some plants are adapted to attract ants?

    F Ants could pollinate the plant's flowers.

    G Ants could farm aphids, which eat the plant's sap.

    H Ants could attack invaders that might eat the plant.

    I Ants could die, adding nutrients to the soil below the plant.

33 A company is planning to build a new factory that uses freshwater pumped from a river to cool its machines while they operate. The company plans on constructing the new factory near an estuary. The freshwater used by the factory will be cooled back to outside temperatures, and then released into the estuary. Which limiting factor would be **most affected** by the building of this new factory?

    A sunlight penetration

    B salt levels in the water

    C nutrient levels in the soil

    D temperature of the water

34 Angie looked under a microscope and saw cells that contain a relatively large structure filled with water. She concluded she was observing a plant cell. Why did she draw that conclusion?

    F She observed a central vacuole.

    G She observed a chloroplast.

    H She observed a lysosome.

    I She observed a nucleus.

35 A group of sheep are grazing in a field. As they eat, the sheep break down the molecules in the grass, which releases energy. Which form of energy is stored in the grass?

    A chemical energy

    B elastic energy

    C nuclear energy

    D thermal energy

36 In the mid 1800s, Charles Darwin described a process called *evolution*. He proposed that organisms changed over time from generation to generation. At first, scientists were skeptical, but they accepted Darwin's idea when new discoveries supported it. Which term describes *evolution*?

    F empirical evidence

    G hypothesis

    H law

    I theory

37 Organisms are grouped with similar organisms. Within groups, there may be other less inclusive groups, which contain fewer types of organisms. Which is the **least** inclusive group that contains both humans and plants?

    A domain

    B kingdom

    C order

    D phylum

38 Jacob has one older brother and one younger sister. He wants to explain relative dating to them using their ages as an example. Which describes their ages using relative dating?

    F Their ages are 14, 12, and 9.

    G They are all about the same age.

    H The boys have different ages than the girl.

    I Jacob is younger than his brother but older than his sister.

39 Alex stirs his pasta sauce on the stove with a metal spoon. He walks away and leaves the spoon in the pot. When he comes back, he grabs the spoon, and it is very hot! Which process took place?

A The temperature of the spoon increased, but its thermal energy does not change.

B Energy in the form of heat transferred from the warmer pot to the cooler spoon.

C The thermal energy of both the pot of sauce and the spoon increased as heat flowed between them.

D The average temperature of the spoon did not change.

40 Sonia investigates where oxygen goes in the body. She observes how oxygen moves from the bloodstream into the cells. Based on this evidence, which structure is Sonia **most likely** to be observing?

F the veins

G the heart

H the capillaries

I the lymph nodes

PLEASE NOTE
- Use only a no. 2 pencil.
- Example: ○ ● ○ ○
- Erase changes COMPLETELY.

Florida Statewide Science Assessment PreparationPractice Test—Form A

Mark one answer for each question.

1 Ⓐ Ⓑ Ⓒ Ⓓ		21 Ⓐ Ⓑ Ⓒ Ⓓ
2 Ⓕ Ⓖ Ⓗ Ⓘ		22 Ⓕ Ⓖ Ⓗ Ⓘ
3 Ⓐ Ⓑ Ⓒ Ⓓ		23 Ⓐ Ⓑ Ⓒ Ⓓ
4 Ⓕ Ⓖ Ⓗ Ⓘ		24 Ⓕ Ⓖ Ⓗ Ⓘ
5 Ⓐ Ⓑ Ⓒ Ⓓ		25 Ⓐ Ⓑ Ⓒ Ⓓ
6 Ⓕ Ⓖ Ⓗ Ⓘ		26 Ⓕ Ⓖ Ⓗ Ⓘ
7 Ⓐ Ⓑ Ⓒ Ⓓ		27 Ⓐ Ⓑ Ⓒ Ⓓ
8 Ⓕ Ⓖ Ⓗ Ⓘ		28 Ⓕ Ⓖ Ⓗ Ⓘ
9 Ⓐ Ⓑ Ⓒ Ⓓ		29 Ⓐ Ⓑ Ⓒ Ⓓ
10 Ⓕ Ⓖ Ⓗ Ⓘ		30 Ⓕ Ⓖ Ⓗ Ⓘ
11 Ⓐ Ⓑ Ⓒ Ⓓ		31 Ⓐ Ⓑ Ⓒ Ⓓ
12 Ⓕ Ⓖ Ⓗ Ⓘ		32 Ⓕ Ⓖ Ⓗ Ⓘ
13 Ⓐ Ⓑ Ⓒ Ⓓ		33 Ⓐ Ⓑ Ⓒ Ⓓ
14 Ⓕ Ⓖ Ⓗ Ⓘ		34 Ⓕ Ⓖ Ⓗ Ⓘ
15 Ⓐ Ⓑ Ⓒ Ⓓ		35 Ⓐ Ⓑ Ⓒ Ⓓ
16 Ⓕ Ⓖ Ⓗ Ⓘ		36 Ⓕ Ⓖ Ⓗ Ⓘ
17 Ⓐ Ⓑ Ⓒ Ⓓ		37 Ⓐ Ⓑ Ⓒ Ⓓ
18 Ⓕ Ⓖ Ⓗ Ⓘ		38 Ⓕ Ⓖ Ⓗ Ⓘ
19 Ⓐ Ⓑ Ⓒ Ⓓ		39 Ⓐ Ⓑ Ⓒ Ⓓ
20 Ⓕ Ⓖ Ⓗ Ⓘ		40 Ⓕ Ⓖ Ⓗ Ⓘ